Selling the book

A BOOKSHOP PROMOTION MANUAL

Selling the book

A BOOKSHOP PROMOTION MANUAL

Edited by Sydney Hyde

CLIVE BINGLEY LONDON

FIRST PUBLISHED 1977 BY CLIVE BINGLEY LTD
16 PEMBRIDGE ROAD LONDON W11
SET BY ALLSET IN 10 ON 13 POINT PRESS ROMAN
AND PRINTED AND BOUND IN THE UK
BY BILLING & SONS LTD OF GUILDFORD AND LONDON

ISBN: 0-85157-513-7

CONTENTS

ACKNOWLEDGEMENTS

The Co-operative Book Trade Fund would like to thank the following publishers and booksellers who made its existence possible during the period 1970-1975:

Associated Book Publishers Ltd
W H Smith & Son Limited
Andre Deutsch Ltd
George G Harrap & Co Ltd
Jonathan Cape Limited
A R Mowbray & Co Ltd
John Murray Ltd
John Menzies (Holdings) Ltd
Macdonald & Co Ltd

The members of the Fund were: Martyn Goff (chairman), Richard Bailey, Michael Hyde, Michael Turner, Jack Stacey, Peter Wolfe.

In various ways, large and small, the Fund notched up a number of achievements. This book is its swan song.

INTRODUCTION

This book is about promotion.

What do we mean by promotion? Briefly it is summed up by our title 'Selling the book'. It is about how to sell books by all the methods at our disposal.

Where the initiative has to come from the publisher, it is an appeal for retailer co-operation, in order to capitalize on the publishers' efforts for the common good. Not only an appeal, but an indication of where and how the retailer can help by adding effort of his own.

Where the promotion effort is entirely in the hands of the bookseller, and the initiative and implementation are his alone, practical advice is given or illustrated.

We have said 'to sell books by all the methods at our disposal'. More specifically, what do we mean by this? For when you arrange books in the window to attract sales, you are indulging in sales promotion. When you re-arrange your stock for the purpose of enhancing sales; when you ring up the retired General to tell him of a new book on military strategy; when you introduce your own named wrapping paper; when you fall in with a publisher's request for a special display; when you circulate the best seller lists from the press among your staff, you are promoting sales; for the motive of all these activities is to sell books. Unless you keep your books in unopened boxes, leave the shop unlighted or unattended, and make no positive attempt to sell your stock, you are bound, however unwittingly, to some extent to be promoting sales.

More specifically, then, we mean furthering book sales by advertising of various kinds, by publicity (including public relations), display, lighting, by book tokens, by riding on the backs of 'juggernauts' such as the book clubs, by constantly seeking out new markets and new customers in the endeavour to sell more books.

There need be nothing 'gimmicky' about sales promotion, which is not to deny that an occasional and specific gimmick does cheer things up and cause the general public to stop, stand, stare and wonder just once in a while. The history of book promotion is well-clad with examples of successful gimmicks for a particular marketing situation. This is all to the good when the time and opportunity are ripe, and provided the thing is executed well enough.

But basically we are talking of ways and means of getting people to know about our shop, to be aware of it, to come into it with reasonable regularity and then to make them want to buy something, to ensure they want to come again, because they like what they find and the way their wants are looked after—in short to see that the shop impresses them.

As far as these regular customers are concerned, it is vital to see that their visits are continually interesting to them, that they enjoy them, find what they want, and find it attractively displayed. Tempt them with the one hand, satisfy them with the other. And reach out as best you may to those people who do not use the shop; adopt means to impress upon them that they should, flatter them by courting their custom. There may not always be a marriage immediately, but some contacts there will be, and stable ones, too, if you continue to solicit and attract their custom and interest.

Promotion is about the tools which lie at your disposal to achieve these ends. They are not tools which you can't afford, but tools which you can't afford not to have and use. Promotion costs less than neglect.

No promotion is good that does not bring profit. Nothing in this book is impractical in purport, nothing is demanded that most booksellers cannot do, however small or short of staff their shops. Not everything in this book will be suitable for every type of bookshop—of course not; but there should be nothing that is not useful to some shop, or which cannot be adapted to meet special market requirements.

So far as bookshops are concerned, a great deal of promotional activity lies in fields that do not require cash—but call for thought, effort and enthusiasm. Much can be done for a bookseller who is prepared to engage in, and be helped in active book promotion, by the originating publisher being willing to do the preparatory work and shoulder the cost of a campaign, or (at worst) only share it. The chapter on publicity is of special value here. When it comes to point-of-sale stimulus, the retailer is mostly reliant on the publisher for his promotional material, to which he must then apply careful, intelligent, imaginative usage.

In this book, point-of-sale promotion is approached from a non-didactic angle, and in a unique way. Historic campaigns, which will be remembered by all present-day booksellers, are cited, in order to give retailers some appreciation of how large campaigns are mounted and financed, and how successes were obtained by booksellers through co-operation with publishers' own ideas—how indeed many booksellers often added their own initiative, enthusiasm and expertise to improve the original schemes.

Display is seen as a vital part of promotion. It is certainly not less, and may well be more important to present the book physically, than to promote it by any other means. It presents a particularly interesting problem to booksellers, for each product is individual in character and is individually and distinctively packaged. Has any other retailer so many competitive products to sell, with so much competing colour on his shelves, arguing and fighting for space and attention?

Tremendous attention has been given to the question of display methods and equipment in recent years, and a good deal of research and costly experiment has been involved. Solutions have been found to many problems, inevitably there can be no ideal formulae, and we have tried to exemplify some of the principal questions here by illustration as well as text.

It is not, therefore, the aim of this book to present promotion as something new, but rather as an integral part of the every-day business of the bookshop!

What may be found helpful is to provide some general review of what can be done and how, and to examine this many-sided subject as a whole. Perhaps, too, a word of warning to any who expect a promotional campaign to induce the instant doubling of sales. A pile of promotional money will seldom—if ever— sell a bad book. Neither will a large promotion budget sell a shop and its products if something is seriously wrong with the shop itself.

Whilst it is not easy to hazard how much booksellers budget for promotion—for it is probably true to say that few booksellers *do* budget for promotion, but rather treat it as something that is coped with when it arises—it is commonly asked by booksellers how much the publisher has spent on a campaign and how he arrived at his proposed expenditure. Though there are many and varied factors that enter into the publisher's calculations, as a general rule of thumb it may be said that he expects to spend on a trade book about 5 per cent of the published price of the book spread over the entire printing. Thus if he prints 4,000 copies of a book published at £2.50, his promotion budget would be in the region of £500.

Of course, there are factors that can cause him to depart from the norm. In addition he will be spending a certain amount on continuing promotion of his back-list, or on books brought suddenly into prominence by some topical event, by a TV series or by all manner of unforeseen circumstances. Thus his overall promotion budget for the year will allow an amount for such contingencies on top of what he envisages as necessary for the new titles in preparation or planned for the year.

While no promotion is good that does not bring increased sales, not all expenditure should be judged by immediate returns. Some expenditure will be incurred in establishing a reputation in areas where the shop is not known, or in wooing customers from districts not immediately adjacent or in the conversion of non-buyers of books into regular customers. This form of promotion must be long-term, and requires patience in assessing its effects. Signs of positive results include new faces in the shop, and demands for books not previously asked for. Keep the staff alert for any indications that your promotional ideas are working. If, at the end of the day, the chickens have not come home to roost, then something was wrong with your initial judgment or with the way the promotion was done. Don't pour good money after bad if you have proof or reason to know that a promotion was a failure; but on the other hand don't condemn sales promotion in the light of one mistake.

This book is intended to encourage promotion, to help you to be successful at it, and to avoid most of the mistakes, and learn by the others.

KEYNOTES

- **Promotion means selling <u>more</u> books**
- **Gimmicks are excellent sometimes; at other times it is attention to detail whether in display, advertising or mail shots that counts.**
- **First tempt; then satisfy.**
- **Promotion works if it increases profit.**

- Promotion is practical.
- Promotion is part of everyday bookshop routine.
- Booksellers should budget for promotion.
- Differentiate between short-term (probably a title) and long-term (the shop itself) promotion.
- Constantly measure both sorts of promotion.

1 ANATOMY OF A NATIONAL CAMPAIGN

By Michael Hyde,
Sales Promotion Director, Wm Collins Sons & Co Limited

The most informative and graphic way of discussing large-scale national campaigns would be to select one of the biggest and most successful of recent years and to reveal how it was conceived, how it was implemented step by step, how it was co-ordinated, how the retailer's requirements were studied, how much it cost and how it succeeded.

After a number of booksellers had been approached, it seemed clear that the promotions most generally commented upon were Collins' Countryside Campaigns, and so it was these campaigns that were chosen as examples. They provide an admirable instance of what can be achieved by publisher-bookseller co-operation, and an indication of the publisher-assistance available to booksellers. It is interesting that as a result of them, books on the subject other than those published by Collins also benefited.

Periodically, a national event or concentrated publicity around a central theme gives publishers and booksellers the opportunity of running a campaign keyed to that subject, and Conservation Year in 1970 provided the very springboard Collins were looking for to mount a national campaign for books on wildlife and conservation. A campaign such as this is useless in itself unless one can subsequently evaluate its success, and in the following pages I shall attempt to set out not only the value of such campaigns in terms of pounds and pence, but also the experience that we have now gained for the long term in establishing new markets.

Over a four-year period Collins mounted two national campaigns on wildlife and conservation, one in 1970 and the second in 1974. The first used the theme *Wildlife in danger*; and the object of the campaign was to involve everyone who had a vested or personal interest in wildlife in our books. The pay-off line of our slogan was *the more you read the more you can do*. 1970 was Conservation Year, and we obviously took full advantage of the national publicity devoted to this subject at the time.

CO-ORDINATING THE MARKETS

The objective was to co-ordinate four distinct markets:

1 Through booksellers to the general public.

2 To schools.

3 Through libraries to increase public awareness among their readers of books on the subject.

4 Through natural history and specialist groups. Forget for the moment that this was a campaign run by an individual publisher—here was a campaign which provided a platform for the exposure of books at every level, from children's books to adult, in hardback and paperback.

Background

For some years Collins have been issuing to schools sets of wallcharts with projects for the older age groups, and colourful wildlife posters with primary schools in mind. The response to this material has indicated a tremendous need and welcome in schools and libraries for visual material of this kind linked with books. Over the four-year period Collins had sold to schools, at 25 pence each, more than 4,000 school-project wallcharts and approaching 6,000 wildlife posters on the following subjects: Birds of the Stream, Woodland Birds, Woodland Flowers, Small Mammals and The Sea Shore.

Budgeting

When budgeting the promotion for a new title we work on approximately 5 per cent of the invoice value of the title. When running a campaign for an entire group of titles, many of which have been available for many years, and where the object is not only to create a new market but to re-establish an existing market, one has to work on estimated extra turnover and on both these campaigns I allowed 10 percent of estimated turnover: 5 per cent for new titles and 5 per cent extra for backlist: plus 10 per cent set against public relations to schools, libraries, etc.

Wildlife in danger 1970

Estimated turnover–£20,000.

Estimated budget on display material including advertising–£2,000. Material for schools, libraries and mailing–£2,000.

The outcome was a turnover of over £31,000. Our total expenditure was £4,310.68.

It can be seen that we exceeded the budget; we also exceeded our turnover expectations to a much greater degree.

Wildlife in danger 1974

Here our object was slightly different, being to sell more books through bookshops, after having established ourselves in the previous campaign through schools and libraries.

This, in turn, meant that we had to budget far more to be spent on display material, promotion incentives, exhibitions, etc. We aimed at an extra turnover of £40,000 and allowed:

Display material and advertising for the trade–£3,000. Exhibitions and exhibition material–£1,000. Schools and libraries (including mailings, author visits, etc–£1,000.

Actual total expenditure was £5, 192.70

Extra turnover was in excess of £49,000.

Let us now examine these two campaigns in detail, considering the object, the problems, the strategy and the results in both the short term and, to a lesser degree, in the long term, which must, for obvious reasons, be somewhat speculative.

WILDLIFE IN DANGER CAMPAIGN 1970

The main problem in the *Wildlife in danger* campaign was how best to draw together all sections of the community, given the comparatively low budget at the outset. So we solicited the help of education authorities, and followed this up by asking for their active co-operation in mailing details of our promotion with their circulars direct to the schools in their areas.

But approaching schools is a comparatively easy matter, given the encouragement of the education authorities. To reach the general public, in the widest sense, is a different matter; and here we needed the co-operation of town councils and civic authorities, requesting their support through museums, libraries and exhibitions held under their own auspices and geared to the subject. In a letter to town clerks, I pointed out that here was an opportunity to draw attention to local and regional conservation problems through exhibitions and media coverage; and I also pointed out the active support we were receiving from schools in their area. It was a piece of gentle and, I believe, acceptable blackmail, which was received with great enthusiasm by many town councils.

Incentives

If we were to expect full co-operation both from the trade and from schools, it was obvious that we should provide some incentives, and so we ran two competitions–a trade window competition for booksellers, and a school-project competition open to all age groups. I will discuss these two competitions in more detail later on.

The phasing of our campaign

Having established our aim, drawn up and agreed our budget, we now planned the actual campaign in four distinct phases.

Phase one: For booksellers it was essential to produce a full-colour display kit suitable for use by large stores, individual retailers and the big chains. Collins guaranteed local advertising to every retailer participating in the campaign, drawing attention to the display in the newspaper of his choice. This, plus the window competition, would give booksellers and their staff sufficient ammunition and enthusiasm to mount the campaign at point of sale.

Phase two: On February 22 I wrote a personal letter to 500 education authorities, enclosing details of our school competition together with a selected list of titles which we felt would appeal to all age-groups. This letter requested their active support and co-operation in circulating our forms and leaflets to schools in their area. By March 3, thirty-nine education authorities had agreed to help, and by the end of May a further twenty-eight authorities mailed schools themselves, three circulated details in school bulletins, and thirteen sent details to us for mailing from London. Altogether 31,500 entry forms and leaflets had been despatched by June 7. The key factor was, of course, that school parties had to visit their local bookseller. The idea in itself was a good one, but the participation of over 1,000 schools and 350 bookshops caused three members of our staff in London a great many headaches in terms of co-ordinating through our representatives schools' visits with booksellers' displays.

Each class-group was invited to visit a local bookshop which displayed a comprehensive range of books on the subject, *Wildlife in danger.* It then had to submit two entries which, in the teacher's opinion, were best in each category. Younger children, aged six to eleven years, had the choice of designing a poster or book jacket on African wildlife, or the British countryside, or pollution in their area, or wildlife in their area. They could use any materials they wished from collage to watercolours. For the eleven-to-sixteen year-olds there was the choice of a suggested newspaper article, or a synopsis of a suggested book on any subject within the terms of the campaign in up to six hundred words.

Phase three: The approach to civic and borough authorities: during the first week in March we wrote personal letters to 520 county and borough councils, informing them of the response from the various educational authorities, and suggesting they run exhibitions highlighting local aspects of conservation through their libraries and civic centres. At the same time we offered assistance with radio, press and television support for any event they felt they could stage in their area. As a result there were twenty-two major exhibitions mounted using the *Wildlife in danger* theme.

Phase four: Having tied together various regional events, we turned to the specialist groups and sent full details of the campaign to more than 200 natural history societies, 500 field study-centres, zoos and national parks, most of which displayed our posters and circulated leaflets to members and associated study groups.

Involving the media

By now the pattern was taking shape, and during phase four we were able to commence our contact with the national and local radio, press and television with a series of press releases which gave a complete breakdown of events scheduled to occur in their areas during the following month. These press releases took the form of news bulletins which were issued weekly. The results included the following programmes and features:

BBC national: Living World, Talk About. *Radio Eirrean.*

Regional radio: Medway, Birmingham, Leeds, Manchester, Oxford, Teesside, Bristol, Blackburn, Humberside.

National press: Financial Times, Times Educational Supplement, The Teacher, Teachers' World.

Television regional: Southern TV, Harlech TV, ATV, BBC Look North.

Press provincial: Birmingham Evening Mail, Manchester Evening News, Chester Chronicle.

Specialist: local natural history society bulletins and specialist natural history magazines.

EXPENDITURE: facts and figures

Display material	2, 219.50
Advertising–trade	244.80
Advertising–press	475.15
Mailing leaflets	509.09
Prizes	200.00
Competition entry forms	193.10
Postage, envelopes, etc	59.54
Selling folders & trade order forms	159.50
Miscellaneous photographs, production costs & art work	250.00
TOTAL	£4,310.68
Estimated turnover	£20,000.00
Actual turnover	£31,000.00

DISCOVER THE COUNTRYSIDE WITH A BOOK FROM COLLINS

Background

This time, in 1974, our main objective was to achieve extra display areas and wider exposure for the books themselves so that the booksellers could take advantage. Once again it was of prime importance to co-ordinate the markets, and we included a further school project competition and new approaches to display material, with the extra dimension of our approaches to district arts associations, zoos etc.

This, we hoped, would bring to a far wider audience an awareness of books on wildlife and conservation apart from a trade competition for imaginative displays and a school project competition to encourage young people's involvement. We decided on a special prize of £150.00 for the most original exhibition geared to our new theme which we hoped would stimulate the interest of museums, natural history societies and libraries.

The mechanics of the operation

Following the same phases as 1970 our first objective was to produce an entirely new approach to a new theme. For booksellers, we devised a flexible type of display material in the form of modular cubes which could be used in any shape or type of display area, from windows to tables to island sites. These again could be flattened to make a series of showcards or erected as cubes to make a window display backed up by window streamers, crowners and full colour posters. Each campaign kit came equipped with a quantity of book lists for mailing to customers and were again backed up by local press advertising at the retailer's discretion.

Over and above the bookshop itself, booksellers were encouraged to mount exhibitions in conjunction with their local authority or natural history society and Collins organised free film shows, author talks, slide lectures and exhibition material and loaned original art work from their range of books for special displays.

EXPENDITURE: facts and figures

The 1974 natural history campaign was even more successful than its predecessor and the results and costs are as follows:

Education authorities mailed with details of the school project competition	242
Education authorities who replied asking for forms for distribution	111
Schools who entered competition	257
Schools asking for free posters	600
Trade press advertising	501.00
Selling folders for representatives in the trade	188.00
Co-operative advertising with booksellers	268.00
Display kits (including full colour modular cubes, sets of full colour wildlife posters and streamers)	2,516.00
Leaflets featuring the entire range of natural history books from Collins	271.00
Exhibition material	678.00
Photographic charges and miscellaneous costs	68.70
Postage costs	52.00

Prizes	450.00
Trips	200.00
TOTAL	£5,192.70
Estimated turnover	£40,000.00
Actual turnover	over £49,000.00

The special exhibition prize of £150 to the organiser of the most original exhibition geared to the theme 'Discover the countryside with a book from Collins' went to the Shrewsbury and District Arts Association.

Extra outlets

There were no less than twenty extra outlets, including zoos, museums and wildlife parks, who co-ordinated displays with their local booksellers. There were five major exhibitions

The first exhibition was launched very successfully on April 29 in conjunction with the Forestry Commission at the *Yorkshire post* building in Leeds, and ran until May 11. The exhibition material consisted of full colour blow-ups in modular form extracted from *The Birds of Britain and Europe; Trees; Butterflies; Animal tracks and signs;* and *The wild flowers of Britain and Northern Europe.*

Gerald Summers was an ideal author to use in our promotion, coming armed with golden eagles, owls, stoats etc. He not only delighted his audience but achieved wide media coverage and was interviewed by BBC 'Look North' and by Leeds radio in 'Radio roundabout'. The *Yorkshire post* gave us considerable editorial coverage before and during the event and ran a children's competition with book prizes from Collins. Attendances were in the region of 6,000. The exhibition was linked to local bookshops in the Leeds area, who gave us window coverage and excellent displays of major titles. The Bollington Festival is staged every four years and ran from May 24 to June 2. E J Morton's bookshops arranged three bookstalls in the marquee for 'Discover the countryside'.

Thorne's bookshop arranged an exhibition at the Hancock Museum of natural history, with supporting displays in the bookshop itself. The exhibition was backed by local advertising, author-talks and other media coverage.

The Shrewsbury and District Arts Association held their winning exhibition with the Nature Conservancy Council and Collins's 'Discover the countryside' campaign at College Hill House. During the exhibition they showed two Collins films, i.e. *Solo* and *In the shadow of man.* There were also slide shows using slides from Collins *Natural history series* and *Field pocket guides*, backed by local advertising and other media coverage.

Finally, Blackwell's mounted an exhibition at the Oxford Motel to highlight Collins 'Discover the countryside' campaign, backed by a display at Blackwell's Bookshop. Various authors gave talks and there was full media coverage and local advertising. The *Oxford Mail* also ran a competition for schools.

What have we learned?

First and foremost that campaigns of this nature, properly co-ordinated, result in extra business. This business can be reflected not only through the order forms we receive from bookshops and repeats we continued to receive for the titles involved long after the campaign was over, but also through our constant correspondence with schools. We are now constantly in touch with no fewer than 600 schools around the country on a regular basis and are stocking their libraries through the trade with a separate section of wildlife and conservation books.

I attribute this not only to the school project competition itself, but also to the fact that the wildlife posters have been an enormous success, particularly amongst primary and secondary schools. Over and above this, however, an interesting fact has emerged in that probably for the first time the national press have become aware of the enormous general interest in books on wildlife. This has been borne out by the current bestseller lists which since our campaign in May 1974 have featured titles such as *The birds of Britain and Europe, The wild flowers of Britain and Northern Europe, Animal tracks and signs* and *Trees of Britain and Northern Europe.*

Direct mail

A simple factual leaflet is all that is required but so often the cost of postage is overlooked when costing the operation. Postage costs can well be in excess of the printed leaflet itself when going to a large market. In the case cited above postage was kept to a minimum by using official bodies and organisations to mail out to their own memberships. If one had attempted to go to the vast, untapped general public with a leaflet, it would have been quite a different story. One would have needed glossy, full-colour brochures, Reader's Digest style, to persuade a new market to take even an interest, and this type of mail presents fearsome problems and prohibitive costs.

Display material

The problem for publishers these days is to provide suitable display material for the vastly differing needs of individual trade outlets. It must be flexible, colourful and space-saving; it must be designed to be used in small areas and also adaptable for exhibition material. But first and foremost it must compete in the market place with highly professional display material designed for the high street by other manufacturers and competitors in the leisure market. Hence a display kit containing a variety of material for such a campaign as outlined above seems to be essential. All too often it is ignored, so that when the market has been alerted, the point-of-sale itself is absent.

Publicity

The media, from newspapers, through television and radio, are there to provide news features and entertainment and often newsmen and producers are starved of valuable material for their own use. It is up to the publisher and the bookseller to keep the media, particularly regional media, constantly alerted as to the type of promotions they are running. With subjects such as conservation, pollution and wildlife, it is a comparatively easy job for the media to relate local problems to books, and they are willing to go to great lengths to promote books if given suitable ammunition. In this the bookseller can play his own part.

The young market

Recent market research surveys have proved that all too often young people are introduced to books as a source of 'fun' and entertainment at primary school level, and then in their secondary school years, books are treated simply as basic tools for learning. The fact that books can provide an essential dimension to their hobbies and a source of entertainment is forgotten. This idea of introducing young people to bookshops, and to books not always available in the school libraries, was an attempt to correct the situation.

One cannot always relate results of marketing campaigns in terms of pounds and pence. Creating a market in the long term is of vital importance, and here we have applied various ideas and produced results; some can be measured and others have yet to be evaluated.

This brings us back to the point about budgets. Obviously we all budget against potential results and at the end of the day work out the profitability of such campaigns; but in these two instances we were looking for greater support by libraries, more involvement by schools, and to increase the media's awareness of books geared to a subject. Here one must work out a budget in terms of future investment, and from Collins's point of view, with a constant flow of new titles in mind. This is where we hope the extra outlets and additional interest from a new public make this type of operation worthwhile to us and, we hope, to the trade as a whole.

KEYNOTES

- **Campaigns must be evaluated: they show the way ahead.**
- **Define the market you are aiming at honestly and sharply; don't soften the impact by trying to appeal to fringe groups.**
- **Enlist the support of town halls, local museums, education committees and public libraries.**
- **Plan your campaign in detail and budget for it accurately.**
- **Never neglect competitions: they involve people actively in a bookshop's promotion.**
- **Keep the local press, the media, education authorities, librarians and others abreast of the campaign by frequent short press releases. Half a page of typed and duplicated facts, enthusiastically presented, will do the trick.**
- **Contact all local societies relevant to the subject of promotion: eg archival, archaeological or historical societies for a history promotion. Initially the same press release will serve; later a more detailed account may be needed.**
- **Be careful to cost posting into any direct mail operation.**
- **Try to distribute leaflets, etc., by other means than the post wherever possible.**

2 BOOKSELLERS' COMMENTS ON 'DISCOVERING THE COUNTRYSIDE'

BLACKWELL'S, OXFORD

By Roger Cole

Blackwell's is principally known as an academic bookshop and has not been noted in the past for any noteworthy inventiveness or effort in the field of general or leisure-appeal bookselling. It was, and is, my opinion that in taking this view we were losing valuable business on an increasing scale to other bookshops in the city and surrounding area, and were unknown or, if known, unwelcoming, to a very large segment of the immediate population outside the university.

Radical changes in attitude therefore needed to be made, both inside the shop and in the field of public relations. Most of these changes, of course, only brought into operation methods which other bookshops had been employing for years, which made them all the more overdue.

The Collins campaign

We felt that one of the things we could try was to take books outside the shop to tie in with meetings of local societies, special events etc, and we had been doing this for some time when we learned about the Collins 'Discover the countryside' campaign. We decided to mount a special exhibition away from the shop to see whether, in a different setting, we could persuade significant numbers of people over a period of days that the academic image, though fine in its place, did not represent all we had to offer.

Location and aims

The exhibition was held at the Oxford Lodge Motel from June 9-12, 1974. Since this was the first exhibition of its type which we had attempted, much of the planning was new to us, and we found a talk with Michael Hyde in London of immense value in sorting out the problems.

We decided that we would aim to interest as wide a cross-section of the public as possible by means of local radio, newspaper advertising, in-shop advertising, posters put up in the city and handbills included with parcels; and as many schools and colleges of advanced learning by direct contact as we could.

Format

The format of the exhibition was to consist of a display of the entire range of Collins Natural History books then available, supplemented by talks by authors and people active in the field of natural history and film shows. Also to participate were the Cotswold Wildlife Park (who took a stand and provided live exhibits) and the World Wildlife Fund (who provided us with a great deal of superb display material). Thus, the final programme was as follows:

June 9	Opening by Johnny Morris.
June 10	Talk am and pm by Richard Mabey. Film shows late afternoon. Evening reception, for local librarians, important interested parties, press etc, to view exhibition and meet Sir William Collins.
June 11	Panel am and pm with the directors of three zoos answering questions. Film shows evening.
June 12	Talk am and pm by Gerald Summers (with vultures and golden eagle). Film shows evening.

Good results

1 We received, as a bookshop, a great deal of free publicity in the local media.

2 We were very pleasantly surprised by the numbers of people who expressed pleasure at and *gratitude* for the exhibition, and who expressed the intention of telling friends, colleagues and relations about it, and about the source of the books.

3 In-shop sales of Collins natural history books quadrupled during June and maintained a higher-than-average sales record right through until

Christmas—a direct result, we feel, of the exhibition. This increase also extended, to a lesser degree, across our entire natural history range, as customers became more familiar with our total stock.

Bad points

1 The siting of the exhibition, was, however unavoidably, wrong. Blackwell's has no separate exhibition facility on the premises, and Oxford as a city is lamentably devoid of suitable accommodation for hire. Our choice of the Oxford Motel, whose Conference room in itself was ideal, was forced upon us by the lack of any other site, but its one major drawback was that it was located on the outskirts of the city.

This lack of a central position meant that walk-in trade, which should obviously be a vital component of such an exhibition, was missing, and is one of the factors which accounts for the poor financial return (£167.05) on the exhibition itself, as opposed to shop sales in the month of June which, as a direct result of the exhibition and its attendant publicity, quadrupled (£2,254.65).

2 Our publicity, though right in its scope, failed badly in some areas, notably newspaper advertising (insufficient, not specific enough, and badly placed) and the handbill/posters, which arrived too late to be properly effective. On this latter point, for example, we were unable to notify schools in proper time with written descriptive material, so that the overall response from them was poor.

Conclusion

We feel that despite the disappointments, which were largely, through inexperience, of our own making, the mounting of this exhibition was of real value to us in many ways.

It was an extremely valuable public relations exercise whose beneficial effects are still being felt. It made a small profit, and it has resulted in in increased sales over a long period; and it brought our name before a large number of people and institutions who might otherwise never have thought of us.

In many ways, peculiar though it may sound, we at Blackwell's went into organising this exhibition as innocents. That we came out on the right side of the balance sheet, and with the feeling that it had been a worthwhile exercise was in no small part due to Michael Hyde and his staff at Collins. It was a venture which we should be very happy to repeat, and we do feel that it was the kind of promotion which benefits a bookshop very greatly.

As far as we are concerned, we have gained a whole new range of customers, broadened the image of the kind of service and stock we provide, proved to ourselves that it does no harm to be a little adventurous once in a while, and, above all, sold a lot of good books.

We have nothing but praise for Collins who proposed an imaginative and original variant on normal run-of-the-mill publishers' promotions, and who backed booksellers to the hilt with superb display material and good advice.

MIDLAND EDUCATIONAL COMPANY

By F J Findlay

The 'Discover the countryside' campaign by William Collins suggested sales promotion ideas that cried out for involvement by the bookseller. We decided to participate as widely as possible and to give maximum backing to the publisher. In addition to supporting Collins's own arrangements, we wrote to 118 schools in the area, inviting them to send parties of children to the shop during the three weeks of the exhibition we were to mount, and advising them that there would be a special feature on the first afternoon.

Animals–live and stuffed

We borrowed several stuffed wild animals from the Birmingham Natural History Museum and filled a window with these and with Collins books on the subject. We mounted a similar in-store display together with a display of photographs from Dudley Zoo, who also ran their own competition based on wild animals.

We arranged a visit from the zoo of a wallaby, a boa constrictor, a Jacob's lamb, an Amazonian parrot, black rabbits and a fox cub; plus, of course, their handlers. This took place on the first afternoon of the exhibition, together with a visit by Phil Drabble, author of *Badgers at my window* and *My beloved wilderness*, a frequent broadcaster and feature writer. Apart from the parrot, which was in a cage, the other animals were free to roam around the shop. The boa constrictor was always with its handler, but was often draped around the shoulders of visiting school children.

Schools

Parties of school children on this first afternoon varied from twelve to forty two in number—a total of 300 children visited the shop between 2 pm and 4.30 pm. Some looked at books, several bought them; they all looked at the animals, and Phil Drabble answered numerous questions put to him by the children.

The following days, we entertained several school parties, sometimes as many as seventy five children at a time. They sat or lay on the floor and looked at books, getting material for their projects. During the three weeks of our exhibition we were visited by over 600 school children, plus several teachers and parents. Every school bought books from us either at the time of their visit or during the following few weeks.

Press publicity

We followed this activity a month later with a page of photographs in a local magazine and a large advertisement on the opposite page. A small three-year old girl who was in the shop with her mother appeared in several press and magazine photographs. We invited her, with her parents, for coffee one morning and gave her copies of the best photographs. She lives on a new estate and, having shown the photographs to her friends, we now have several new young customers.

Repeats

We repeated this exhibition for National Book Week but without the live animals. We ran our own competition in association with William Collins and the Natural History Museum in Birmingham. We were visited on this occasion by Gerald Summers, author of *Lure of the falcon* who brought a few of the rare birds from his sanctuary, including his golden eagle.

Conclusion

We considered these promotions so successful that we repeated them in 1973 and 1974, again in association with William Collins. The results have proved worthwhile, people still talk to us about them, ask us when the next one will be held. We think we have helped to create a wider interest in this subject and, because of this, we sell more books relating to conservation of the countryside.

PHILIP, SON & NEPHEW LIMITED

By Stuart Smith

In order to ensure the maximum value from a promotional idea, it must be presented in depth. A gay poster promotes a book, but only to those who happen to see it–usually in the bookshop. It may catch the eye and promote an instant response in interest in that book, and if the customer is standing beside the title he may pick it up to look at it or even buy it.

Advertising in depth

This is where the Collins 'Discover the countryside' campaign can be quoted as a step in the right and admirably practical direction. Here we had some attempt at advertising in depth. Firstly take a subject–not a title–this widens the scope for grouped display, offers an assortment of title and price, and in this case can be linked with national projects in the nature and ecology fields.

Secondly it can be directed to the young through the schools as a 'Further reading' project, and by circulating the schools and the bookshop at the same time, provide several interesting 'spin-off' possibilities–such as encouraging the young into the shop and offering new vistas of adult books.

A broad approach

This system provides a reassured and definite promotional approach to what must be one of the most interested sections of the community as far as a 'nature' subject is concerned. After all no one tries to advertise drink in a temperance journal, but any big city bookseller will confirm the fascination that nature and birds in particular hold for the thousands of children who rarely see a bird other than sparrows and pigeons in their scene of concrete and brick. Though much of the style of 'Discover the countryside' would seem to be directed at the young, it can equally be directed at the adult who, influenced by the media, is already interested in ecology and preservation.

Conclusion

Could this promotion be a possible pilot or pattern for other publishers and many other subjects such as gardening, cookery, sport and so on? The writer is one bookseller who certainly hopes so.

KEYNOTES

- **The publisher's Publicity Director or Manager is very skilled in methods of promotion. Don't hesitate to ask his advice before planning a campaign.**
- **Simple leaflets in customers' parcels and/or statements is one of the cheapest forms of advertising.**
- **A campaign or exhibition opened by a nationally known figure gives both a tremendous send-off. A photograph of a celebrity plus a couple of sentences from him draws attention to an exhibition of almost any size or shape to people who would normally not notice it.**
- **Choose the most central site possible for an exhibition. Remember that a temporarily empty shop (between lettings)**

can often be obtained for a fortnight's exhibition at low cost.

- See if your local museum or art gallery can lend you relevant materials.

3 PROMOTION: POINT-OF-SALE

For this section, much of which is concerned with point-of-sale display, five booksellers, representative of the retail trade as a whole, were invited to state briefly what they regarded as the basic 'golden rules'. Comparisons are interesting and instructive to booksellers and publishers alike.

BOOKSELLER A

1 Place where it will be seen.

2 Make sure colours stand out from their background.

3 Make sure, periodically, that the material is not shoddy or tatty or falling to pieces through handling or wear and tear.

4 Keep well topped-up (if counter-pack or dump-bin).

5 Do not leave too long in the same place if seen to be unsuccessful. Experiment with different positions.

6 Do not let it jar with surroundings (eg do not advertise *The joy of sex* in or near your Theology section).

7 Take into account, when using point-of-sale material, your knowledge of your customers. If you are in a conservative area, for example, you may make more enemies than friends if you use questionable material. Always remember your knowledge of likely local benefits from such advertising; do not be beguiled or misled by publishers who enthuse about the nationwide picture.

8 Do not be satisfied, necessarily, with what you think you *have* to have. If you have proved to a publisher in the past that you are prepared to work for him, you will find that he is happy to reciprocate, and will prepare special material to your own individual specification.

BOOKSELLER B

1 Each display should be dominated by one over-riding theme.

2 Full use should be made of *all sales aids* such as showcards, stands, posters, counterpacks and dump-bins.

3 Point-of-sale material should be designed to create a demand and to reinforce a dormant demand.

4 All forms of dispenser should be strong and not fall apart after the sale of the first two or three books. Their size must be sensible!

5 Any message should be concise and have 'punch'.

6 Cards and posters should have regard to booksellers' lack of available wall space at eye-level and therefore modest in size; although window show material may on occasion be larger.

Window

1 Display should be designed to stop the passer-by in his tracks.

2 Should have a compelling focal point, with lines of display directing to this point.

3 Must be stable.

4 Must make full use of window space and yet be uncluttered.

5 Should have architectural form with intelligent use of symmetry and contrast.

6 Should have an eye to Colour, Texture, Lighting and, occasionally, Incongruity.

Interior

1 Know the best-selling points inside the shop.

2 Support the window display with interior showing of same titles.

3 All titles visible and plenty of face forward display.

4 New titles immediately visible on entering shop.

5 Classify logically.

6 Signal subject sections clearly.

BOOKSELLER C

1 Don't overcrowd the shop with advertising matter.

2 Site it so that it can be clearly and easily seen.

3 Do not obscure part of the card or cut-out with stock, so hiding the title of the book and sales message.

4 Don't leave the blank side of the card uncovered if it is going to be visible. Back it with another card or hide the blank side.

5 Make sure that it remains clean and in good condition. Remember showcards can warp or become defaced or faded.

6 When using posters or streamers make sure that they are securely fixed and do not bulge or sag or flap about. If they show signs of tearing take them off display immediately.

7 Keep a special eye on the material in the window: take care to see it is not fading or fly-blown.

8 Secure the material firmly. Don't lean cards feebly against books or fixtures and hope for the best. If they are doing a job for you, they deserve to stand up for themselves!

9 Animation is good and attracts. Where appropriate, make good use of it; but remember production is often 'shaky', so be sure that displays stand up to wear and tear.

10 If what the publisher has provided does not fit in with your requirements don't be afraid to improvise or adapt it to your needs by using it in part or by cutting up and remounting.

BOOKSELLER D

I must confess I find it difficult to describe what I consider good point-of-sale publicity from publishers. In my view too much clutter is a bad thing, but often packs of fast-selling paperback ephemera do well on cash desks; so I would make the following my rules:

1 Important new books seldom need it, especially if they are of a serious nature.

2 Stick-on publicity of the elusive 'psycho' type—I mean where the title is not even mentioned—I simply deplore.

3 I consider a solid card from a publisher setting out clearly the facts about a series or, for instance, a biography that is appearing in several volumes, to be useful.

4 Cased packs of paperbacks of an ephemeral nature are useful as they can sit neatly on the cash desks without getting in anyone's way. Also they are sometimes big enough to stand up on the floor. Good examples of the above are New English Library's standing pack to hold four by six copies of *Art of Walt Disney*; the Quartet Books similar standing pack holding seven by three copies of the paperback edition, plus one copy of the hardback, of *The joy of sex*; the Petersburg Press small pack, carrying six copies of David Hockney's *Fairy tales of the brothers Grimm*—very effective; and the Quartet Books standing pack to hold twelve by six copies of *The Queen and I.*

BOOKSELLER E

1 Avoid monotony in shelf display by:

a Facing a proportion of books with eye-catching jackets.

b Varying the space between shelves.

c Using sloping display shelves to take faced copies, especially large illustrated books and art books.

2 Resist temptation to show too many books in the window, thus losing impact. The window is best used for gaining the interest of a potential customer not for showing the size and range of your stock. A window with a clear view through to the interior of the shop will do this more effectively.

3 While the arrangement of a shop is to some extent dictated by size and available space it should never be assumed that there is no scope for flexibility. The switching of sections within the general framework often stimulates sales and reminds assistants of available stocks. Books need moving from time to time as they have a tendency to grow into the walls.

4 Good lighting, which can be used where necessary to emphasize special displays, is essential.

5 Sections should be clearly and sufficiently labelled.

6 A children's department, particularly, needs sales aids such as posters, mobiles and toys, to create the right atmosphere of informality and to intrigue the children themselves. We find that little wicker chairs, with brightly coloured cushions are very popular with the younger children.

7 The judicious use of free publicity material from publishers and Book Tokens goes without saying; but we feel that it is also important to emphasize the position of a bookshop as a focal point in a local community. Thus we display concert and theatre posters as well as those issued by the local authority. We have a number of poster-size backgrounds of plate glass fixed to the walls, to which posters and notices can be easily fixed.

8 Encouragement should be given to staff to produce ideas and carry them out effectively.

KEYNOTES

- **Refresh displays frequently. Marked books, torn jackets and dented showcards must be replaced.**
- **Use all sales aids.**

- Keep messages short and punchy.
- Window displays should be echoed in the shop whenever possible.
- Check that displays are firm. Cards lopsidedly placed against books look messy and off-putting.
- Put at least a small proportion of shelved stock face out.
- Don't overcrowd the window. It should give some idea of the range of stock and invite passers-by to come and see the rest.

4 PROMOTION: SIX CASE HISTORIES

It was thought that the best way of discussing the matter of publicity and in particular of the place of point-of-sale in selling efforts would be to take a number of case histories, examine what was done, how it was done, how it was received and what results were obtained. Thus, six booksellers were each invited to select a campaign for a book or series that they regarded as outstanding.

These booksellers were representative of major cities, country towns, provincial suburbs, etc. They were asked, when making their choice, to bear in mind the quality and effectiveness of the point-of-sale material supplied, the quality and extent of the back-up publicity and the degree of consideration of the retailers' needs and also, of course, the resultant sales.

Publishers were invited to quote costs where possible as it was thought useful and perhaps educative for those at the retail end to have some idea of the money involved in the various activities concerned. The books are not included here in any particular order.

GEORGE BEST: AN INTIMATE BIOGRAPHY

By Michael Parkinson (Hutchinson)

The bookseller's comments were that it was a typical example of how a book can be made to sell if the publicity is loud enough. 'Immoral I call it', he adds, but those who know this popular and successful bookseller would not expect him to restrain his sense of humour, combined always, it must be said, with shrewdness and a very large measure of commonsense.

Hutchinson describe their campaign below and add, what is generally accepted, that it proved highly successful.

The selling technique for this book was planned on two fronts: a sales promotional campaign based on a two-colour insert in the *Bookseller* eight weeks before publication, and a PR campaign including a tour of nationwide regional centres in the week prior to publication.

'The *Bookseller* insert was designed as a loose six-page brochure/poster, for which a total of £600 was spent on production (including photography, preparation of artwork and printing). An additional £225 covered the cost of insertion in the January 18th issue. The insert served both as an announcement of publication and as a poster for bookshop use. An extra 3,000 copies were printed simultaneously and were utilised as window and other display material. With the addition of some £25 for dry-mounting costs, the total expenditure for this side of the campaign came to £850.

'The PR tour, during which Michael Parkinson and George Best were accompanied by publicity manager Jeremy Cox, consisted of visits to Manchester, Leeds, Glasgow and London. In addition, a publication party (sponsored by Martini) was held at Martini Towers. The tour resulted in more than 500 column inches of national and provincial media coverage, including both interviews and feature articles, plus over a dozen television and radio appearances. The PR expenditure amounted to £650.

'The total expenditure on this title was £1,500. Twenty thousand copies of the book were printed; in the first three months after publication, more than three quarters of the print run was sold.'

THE OXFORD BOOK OF CHILDREN'S VERSE

Edited by Iona and Peter Opie (O U P)

The bookseller commented that in the general view of his staff, this was certainly one of the most successful recent promotional campaigns.

'The showcard was excellent. There was a really mouth-watering prospectus and this was well supported by generous press, radio and TV publicity. It was potentially a good seller, but we sold many more than we should have expected to because of the splendid promotion.

'It had a first rate jacket that undoubtedly sold copies. The whole promotion was an incentive to the staff to get behind the book. They did, with great success.'

The publisher comments: 'The Oxford book of children's verse, edited by Iona and Peter Opie, was published on May 17, 1973. The first printing was 20,000, plus 10,000 printed in the USA for OUP New York. Two years later the UK printings for sale everywhere in the world except the USA totalled about 55,000; and we had supplied the same quantity again to

Book Club Associates. OUP New York had printed a total of 22,000. Sales from them continue to flourish.

'Our advertising expenditure totalled £1,150, which seemed to us modest. We gave away 150 review copies to journals, radio, and television in this country and Europe. From this investment of books a huge file of review clippings resulted. There were also feature articles resulting from interviews with the Opies in: *Daily telegraph magazine, Observer magazine, The times, Sunday times, Liverpool daily post, Times educational supplement, Mother and baby, New York times.*

'There were television interviews on: South Today (BBC Southern Region), Day by Day (Southern TV), Nationwide (BBC 1), Good Afternoon (Thames TV) and radio interviews on Kaleidoscope, Today, Woman's Hour, Late Night Extra, BBC Radio Solent, World of Books (BBC External Services), Dateline London (BBC External Services).

'We used the jacket illustration on all the printed publicity for the book, and also as the cover for our Spring list that year.

'We produced a prospectus, of which 56,000 were printed at a cost of £600. About 6,500 of these were supplied to our overseas branches; 5,000 were mailed to the trade and libraries, 12,000 to schools; and 24,000 were supplied to booksellers for their own mailings. Besides this we produced two statement stuffers, one advertising the Opie book alone (60,500 printed), the other combining this book with another anthology (22,500 printed). The total cost of producing both these was £750. A window sticker was also produced.

'The other display aid we produced was a red-plastic, single-copy display stand. It says simply "The perfect gift from Oxford University Press"; so though we got it out especially for the *Book of children's verse,* it can be used for any suitable Oxford book.

'A postage frank advertising the book was used on all post going out from OUP offices for a month about publication time.

'One of the most time-consuming parts of the launching campaign was the exhibition we mounted at the National Book League. It was entitled 'Three Centuries of Nursery Rhymes and Poetry for Children'. Over 800 items were displayed, drawn from the Opie collection. We opened it on the publication day of the book with a press party that launched both book and exhibition. It involved the printing of a catalogue, a poster, and invitations, but there is no doubt that it brought quite a lot of extra publicity to the book, mentions in 'forthcoming events' features, and more interviews than would probably have been arranged for the book alone. The Puffin Club arranged an outing to the exhibition and there were a number of school parties.'

RIDER BOOKS PROMOTION

Rider Books Limited

Selected by a prominent and distinguished Midlands bookseller, who says that 'Riders' Comparative Religions' serves as an example of a particularly imaginative campaign. The point-of-sale material was highly praised and held to be outstandingly good, producing sales that might have been regarded as surprising for books of this nature but for the high merit of the promotional campaign generally.

The publisher described his campaign as follows:

'In the spring of 1974 it was decided for the first time to have a general imprint promotion for Rider books. An eighty per cent increase in Rider turnover confirmed the promotion's success. With the help of a survey, conducted by Hutchinson representatives, to determine which features of the campaign were most productive, a similar promotion was planned for 1975. As before, it was designed to generate both trade and consumer interest.

'This year's trade promotion consisted of a shelf talker, a window sticker a representative's folder to consolidate the various features of the campaign, and an attractive four-colour poster with a dual purpose. The poster served as a promotion piece for the imprint, with all advertising copy printed on the back, and was also offered in packs of ten for re-sale as a decorative hanging. (Bookstore response to the latter was so positive as to render the poster largely self-liquidating). Trade promotion costs came to £2,050.

'To reach the general and young people's markets, some £400 were spent for radio spots. Space advertising in *Time out* and the arts page of *The Guardian* served as back-up, at a cost for space and production of £1,000. In addition, a direct mail campaign was launched to promote the poster to institutions of higher education. Together with distribution costs for the poster, this amounted to another £170.

'Thus a total of £3,620 was spent on the 1975 Rider imprint promotion. Results are once again encouraging. More than 14,500 books were ordered, representing an increase of 30 per cent over last year's sales total. As a result of the promotion, ninety four new accounts were taken on as stock-holding customers supporting the imprint.'

JENNIE

By Julian Mitchell (Collins)

The bookseller chose this because it was an outstandingly successful book. Again, it was instanced as a book that achieved its success because of topical factors and able and tireless publicity, rather than through the qualities of the book itself. The posters and showcards were excellently designed and admirable from the retailers' point of view.

Collins comment modestly:

'It would be nice to claim that the success of *Jennie* was due entirely to the performance of Collins publicity and sales departments, but unfortunately we must admit that the incredible sales of the book (which was very much a package to coincide with Thames Television's series) were largely due to the fact that the book and a full credit was shown for fifteen seconds at the end of each of the episodes. The series consisted of seven one-hour plays shown at peak time throughout the late autumn, running up to Christmas. The timing was, from our point of view, perfect and it put *Jennie* straight to the top of the bestseller list.

'Promotion was very much a combined effort between Thames TV and ourselves, so it is hard to evaluate in terms of costs. Collins spent approximately £1,000, split evenly between full colour posters and showcards; and £500 on the typical Christmas tombstone-style advertisements which served, probably, as no more than a reminder to the public.

'We put a lot of effort though into pre-sale to the trade, by use of a brochure produced basically by Thames with some assistance from ourselves. A copy of this was sent to every one of our accounts, three months prior to publication. A series of extracts from the programmes was shown around the country in key centres–Birmingham, Manchester and London– at booksellers' gatherings. These did much to stimulate the booksellers' enthusiasm and confidence, resulting in a very large subscription. Again, though, we doubt if they would have been so willing to support us had they not enjoyed such a success with *World at war* the previous year.'

OCTOPUS BOOKS

Octopus Books Limited

The Octopus Books Christmas campaign was chosen by a large bookseller in a northern town. It was, he said, incredibly successful, and lifted the sales of Octopus Books beyond expectation and has maintained them there. The material supplied was excellent, well suited to bookshops and it was, therefore, liberally displayed throughout the shop. To his mind it was one of the most successful operations and, with co-operation and support from the bookseller, paid off handsomely.

The publisher comments:

'£60,000 was spent on this promotion and that money was used, not only in producing the television commercial and buying the 'time', but also paid for 40,000 copies of an illustrated leaflet, posters, crowners, window stickers, and showcards, and some trade advertising.

'Although, generally, 1974 was considered a good year for book sales, Octopus Books' turnover in the UK increased by 110 per cent, and this must be attributed in part to this promotion.

'The promotion was so successful that we are going to do something similar for next Christmas.'

SHARDIK

By Richard Adams (Allen Lane)

This recommendation came from a bookseller in a County town well-known for his enterprise, enthusiasm and energy. He had no doubt about his choice and his praise for the publisher's promotion was unstinted.

'The display material was splendidly conceived; there was good variety to suit any type of shop and it met all limitations imposed by individual structure and space. It was very adaptable and not only produced results in sales, but attracted favourable comments from customers. The effect of the promotion continued long after the initial impact.'

Allen Lane say of the campaign:

'*Shardik*, the second novel by Richard Adams, was published in November 1974. The book had the advantage of following one of the greatest publishing phenomena of the twentieth century, yet it was necessary to establish its own individuality and more adult appeal. Allen Lane mounted a major national promotion campaign.

'Point-of-sale material was designed in display kits and consisted of a fold-out showcard, window streamer, bookmark and bookmark-holder, each reproducing the image of the bear Shardik, which complemented the visual impact of the book jacket. In addition, and where appropriate, a photograph of the author and a list of characters (for this is a complicated book) were included. These kits were distributed with subscription orders for the book and supplied on request to individual booksellers. The total cost of producing this material was approximately £2,500.

'Advertising was carried out over a period of six months, from pre-publication trade advertisements in August and September, to publication day in the nationals, through the Christmas supplements and W H Smith Christmas selection; and again, in the trade press and nationals, when the reprint became available at the end of January 1975. Here again, the bear was the main image in each advertisement; and our expenditure, including setting, designing and block-making, was in the region of £1,900.

'The other major item, although by no means equivalent in terms of expenditure, was individual promotions, which included a dinner for Richard Adams and selected guests from the trade and press at the Travellers Club, and travelling and entertaining expenses for signing sessions. These took place at Hatchards in London, John Prime's in Kings Lynn, The Red House Bookshop in Thame and Blackwell's in Oxford. These sessions were enormously successful and resulted in average sales of more than 400 copies. We provided the usual back-up for these occasions, including leaflets for Hatchards and Blackwell's, and local advertising in the *Oxford mail, Evening standard, Times,* etc.

Estimates put total expenditure by Allen Lane on the *Shardik* promotion at approximately £4,700. In return, we received full co-operation from the booksellers who used the point-of-sale material to full advantage; and they very patiently waited for the second printing, as the book sold out within two weeks of publication. Prominent review and feature coverage on the book itself, and on the Richard Adams phenomenon, also contributed considerably to the book's success.'

KEYNOTES

- Celebrity authors' visits to bookshops create sales.
- Media PR, local or national, is a positive selling aid.
- An exhibition connected with a book usually leads to considerable increase in media mentions.
- Tie up books and TV or radio series.

5 PROMOTION: PAPERBACKS

By Paul Chevalier
Executive Director (Promotion), Pan Books

This section presented certain difficulties in that necessarily some parts of it cover ground dealt with under other sections on, for instance, PR, display, point-of-sale, publicity. As paperbacks form a vitally important part of any bookshop, and of the publishing scene, and so often call for separate treatment and merchandising techniques, it was felt right to leave this as an entity despite some inevitable duplications elsewhere. Anyway, duplication of important points is no bad thing; neither, for that matter, are differences of viewpoint on some matters, however basic.

Objects of impulse

Studies made of patterns of paperback purchase have always shewn that a staggeringly high percentage remains triggered by impulse. Desirable, or not, it's a well-documented fact; and paperback publishers have learned to live with it. They knew it back in the days when paperbacks–then not quite 'respectable'– were sold from wind-swept tables in the doorways of high street booksellers. They must still contend with it now that the same booksellers, after successive rearguard-actions, adjustments of policy and layout, have largely surrendered themselves and their customers to the lure of the paperback.

It has been a remarkable fifteen-year process, contested by many booksellers from the outset and by not a few even today. But it only ever had one possible outcome–complete acceptance of the paperback by all sections of the bookbuying market. And though it sounds sacrilegious to some, the consumer–now eager for paperbacks 'as if appetite had grown by what it fed on'–and still buffeted by impulse, continues to emphasise one rudimentary marketing principle for the industry: he doesn't buy to a plan or a discriminating need, he selects from what is put in front of him.

People buy what they see on sale?

Is it true? With reservations, and applied especially to general fiction and non-fiction, yes, it is. Confronted with the impressive, colourful choice of hundreds of paperbacks on face-out display, with quotations from reviews, and punch-lines, the consumer does not, for the most part, turn away because he had something different in mind when he came in. Usually, he succumbs. If you accept, then, that the paperback customer is a creature of impulse, can the basic premise be pursued further? Is it true that the more you display, the more they buy? It hardly needs confirmation. The bigger the display the better the sale, is a rule that holds good in most marketing situations. Oddly enough, only in the bookselling trade is it sometimes forgotten. Paperback publishers can attest, too, that they always welcome competition. Their lines thrive best in an almost carnival atmosphere of attraction and counter-attraction. Display is most effective where display is the rule, rather than the exception.

This element of glittering choice has, then, become the key to successful paperback marketing. No-one has so far overdone this to a point where an embarrassment of attractions and displays becomes counter-productive. So however different the rules may be in the hardcover world what makes paperbacks sell is mass display or, in other words, racking.

Racking is the key

All kinds of racking have been produced, tested and scrapped over the years. Driven by fierce competition and the uncomfortable economics of their trade, and conscious of the need to prove their case that a good paperback line shows *more* than the average income yield per square foot of floor space occupied, the publishers have been constantly worrying over the problem of display versus floor space. The end result of it all is probably the K5 system of racking. It uses minimum floor space, but yields remarkable display per foot-run result.

Such racking *is* promotion at the first level. The author new to paperback, seeing forceful PR and point-of-sale campaigns for his rivals, might wonder 'What are they doing for me? ' Two quick answers are 'Using a fifty-man sales force to give you distribution all over the country' and 'Putting your book into K5'. That alone is a powerful start. Until recently, paperback racking, paid for from the promotion budget, was fitted free, more or less, for retailers willing to convert. But faced with annual bills in the order of £50,000 and more, publishers have become more canny. The money is still counted as a promotional cost, but K5 and ancillary systems are now available on 'advantageous terms' (perhaps 50 per cent of cost, depending upon how the footage is allocated, the difficulties of the installation, whether classification is to be used or not, with what safeguards, etc).

The K5 and ancillary systems

WHS, Boots and other multiples, of course, have their own racking systems, similar in many ways. K5 though, is supremely versatile in adapting to the most difficult shop shell contours. It is speedy in installation, hardy, and always available. Used with its island units and modern spinners, it can maximise sales, while at the same time creating both stunning display and attractive walk-through sections.

On classification, within such paperback areas, publishers remain anxious. They have nothing but praise for it where stock-control systems are effective and the staff experienced. But the alternative, arrangement by publisher, does mean that the experienced sales representative can control his section himself; can see at a glance how well or otherwise display is being handled, what needs changing up, re-stocking, abandoning, exploiting. And he has a nationwide pattern of sales reporting to guide him in this.

Know your market

Personal attitudes to stock sometimes obscure the main chance for retailers—perhaps more than in any other business. It's always tempting to believe that one's personal preference in books should also interest others. But for a retailer it can be an expensive mistake and, unless he knows his stock in detail, one that may be slow to emerge.

There's no profit in trying to do the right thing in the wrong area. Any shop must cater to the trade it has. This doesn't mean stagnation. New lines *should* be tried—and thoroughly. They could yield more than those which the manager has come to accept as right for his trade. Paperback houses are more than ready to help make such trials painless with hundreds of titles which can't all be stocked in even large outlets, they are equally concerned not to have the wrong selection on display. But experiments must be monitored carefully and unprofitable series ruthlessly uprooted, however worthy they may appear to be.

One sound way to move forward is by personal recommendation. The manager who goes out of his way to know his customers and their tastes, and to infect them with his own enthusiasm is building in a reliable growth factor. It's yet another form of promotion; slower, but reliable.

Merchandise

The most common cry of the trade is that there isn't room for merchandising. It's often reiterated by an assistant standing within six feet of a year-old poster, a counter pack which has remained half-empty for months, a window sticker it is too much trouble to remove and racking which has never been sullied by anything so brash as a shelf-talker.

Generally, the modern outlet hasn't too much space to play with. But there's always some; and using it well creates extra sales.

Paperback sales soar in an atmosphere of excitement. There's a similarity here with the film industry, now rebuilding itself after years of self-indulgent 'knowing better than the customers'. But even with the wrong product, the film industry had, and has, a masterly approach to selling: in announcing the arrival of a new epic; making known its content and appeal; and carrying right through to the high street the facts about its availability to an audience. Imagine even a moderately good picture arriving unheralded at a local cinema without benefit of posters, front-of-house display, local newspaper advertisements and much more. By contrast, many big sellers—entertainment of exactly the same order—end up in an inconspicuous pile at the local bookseller; unsung in the window, unmarked in the shop by point-of-sale or any other sign of its welcome arrival.

The grocery trade does it right, too. And paperback houses steadily borrow their ideas. Dump bins, shelf talkers, overhead banners, crowners—all are from the restless world of the supermarket, where the special offer, cut price or bargain-of-the-week, constantly coerce the customer. It may be brash, but it works.

Take part

This sense of excitement and opportunity is all too rare in the book trade. In a large branch of a major chain in a cathedral city, an assistant told me recently that she hadn't heard of, and didn't have in stock, an important novel—the film of which had opened locally to unprecedented business. Not her fault, but the manager's. A major film release can sell hundreds of extra copies, even of a book which has been 'out' for years. It *demands* display.

An opportunity to maximise sales should never be lost. A film, a play, an exhibition, an art show, poetry reading, lecture—all can be sales stimulants for the retailer on his toes. Something happens outside the shop? Get both the event and the shop into the local paper. A horticultural show usually stirs gardeners to new effort, so display all the gardening books in stock. Tie in with the organisers and give them a window for the week. Be *in* all such local events. Take part; invite local librarians, teachers, societies and other groups in. Cash in on *anything* which can influence sales. Apart from sales related to the events they sponsor, more and more people will identify with the bookseller outside their specialist interests.

Find out what's being read on the radio, locally and nationally. Be alert to rising TV successes and have the tie-in book out on display at the *peak* of interest. Be *attuned* to what customers are thinking, doing, seeing, reading.

Point-of-sale

Paperback publishers produce the most lavish point-of-sale, and the most ingenious. They're ahead of you—in that cards for current TV and film successes are always in stock. Big promotions are usually accompanied by whole ranges of material. Use them! If it isn't the right size, don't throw it away. Cut it up, improvise. If it *can't* be used feed that information back to the producers. They'll be delighted with your interest. But the record shows that most are ahead of the trade. Some retailers may be able to remember the first dump bins, years ago. Retailers complained they were unsteady, cluttering, an easy target for dogs. It may be so. But years later, the dump bin is a *must* for the big paperback seller. Retailers of all kinds everywhere now use them regularly. Big shops will use as many as six at once.

Another example is the current two-year struggle over counter packs. Many booksellers failed to see their usefulness. Some saw them simply as packing material, to be thrown away on arrival. Lately, the counter pack is coming into its own as a way of creating an important *second* display, *out* of the racks. And for books of specialist interest or special format, they're invaluable.

Point-of-sale is important to paperbacks—more so than advertising, the cost of which is rarely justified by paperback prices and profit margins. Much money *is* spent, though, on the more subtle forms of advertising—in specialist journals, and on booklists, catalogues, exhibition work, etc. More recently, some houses are experimenting with radio commercials which *may* prove to be cost-effective.

Press handling

It has taken too long, but the last two years have seen a complete about-face in press attitudes to paperbacks. Some nationals and their literary editors hold out still, but most have realised that paperbacks are what their own readers mostly buy. In consequence, the press offices of large publishers are deeply committed to close relationships with almost every paper in the country, from nationals, through provincial dailies to the county weeklies. Able to afford some degree of review service to them all, they deal directly with the features editor, the health, science, gardening, women's interest and other specialists; the diarists, picture editors—anyone for whom an angle is apparent. The result is a flood of editorial cover far in excess of what it would be possible to buy.

At the same time, TV and radio programmes of all kinds are steadily using books and authors in various ways. They're willing to feature travellers, historians, psychologists, environmentalists—anyone with something to say. An interdependence has grown up around the realisation that paperbacks are news, entertainment, education, argument. The day of the review squib is over, and the day of the half-page feature is already here. It costs time and money to effect, but it's done so professionally that the film industry is the only real rival for entertainment space of this kind.

Create events

The process is best seen at work in the local paperback events. When a best-selling author arrives in town, not only the local papers, but the TV and radio are more than keen to participate with paperbacks. The weight of their publicity can be shared by the retailer who creates events. Personal appearances and signing sessions are not only immediately good for business; they bring a shop into the limelight, make the local people aware of it and bring them back again and again.

This, too, is a field being pioneered by paperbacks. The coast-to-coast tour , with stops for TV, radio and newspaper interviews (all capitalised upon by local advertising by the shop) is an operation which the sophisticated press offices of the paperback industry handle superbly.

On one such recent tour, a husband and wife team were taken to ten major cities in twelve working days, scoring thirteen TV interviews (for which,film footage of their adventures had been specially prepared in three-minute segments, all different and all exclusive), and countless press and radio interviews. Booksellers were delighted, the more so because most had a visit from the authors. Costs were far less than for one quarter-page in one national newspaper; but the results were fifty times more effective. Alongside such operations, the old-style reliance on reviews looks very feeble.

Tailored promotion

Together with their willingness to offer such events, paperback houses are realising that they must go still further. The 'tailored' promotion is the result. It may be a full-scale exhibition of every title under an imprint, using special stands; and set up, dressed and publicised by the publisher's merchandising, display and press office sections. Or, very differently, it could be the extension of a 'scheduled' major promotion into a major in-store attraction centring on a local or seasonal event.

Giving over a complete shop to overall display to tie in with the arrival of a major film, is one kind. Another example might be in, say, a departmental store's desire to use the colour and background of a best-selling novel to create a store-wide 'theme' for sales. In such cases, the paperback house is willing to go far beyond supplying the regular point-of-sale material–putting cash, material and personnel into window dressing, finding props, and so on. This, too, is an expensive business, but most would count it worthwhile if enthusiasm, facilities and self-help are forthcoming from the retailer.

Some of the most exciting work in this field is being done by special children's publicists recruited by paperback publishers. Local children's book groups' tea parties, competitions, library, park and school events, are filling their work-diaries. Ideas from booksellers in this connection are eagerly welcomed.

Paperback?

Paperback is a term which no longer has any special connotation of price, size or quality. Price barriers collapse every month. Paperbacks being produced now are upright, landscape and almost any size. They utilise full-colour, art paper and special boards, and convert the most expensive coffee-table book to soft-covers without dropping anything except the price. This is the real revolution of the industry. It is already in progess. When the smoke clears away, the retailer who hasn't recognised the scope, appeal and promotional potential of paperbacks may find that catching up is no longer possible. The time to take paperbacks seriously is *now.*

KEYNOTES

- **Paperbacks are bought largely on impulse.**
- **The bigger the display, the greater the sale.**
- **Paperbacks should be classified by subject where the staff is knowledgeable; racked by publisher in other cases.**
- **Scrap slow selling lines and replace with known winners.**
- **Don't be afraid to be brash in displaying paperbacks.**
- **Check what is being read on the radio or serialised on television.**
- **Point-of-sale counts in paperback selling.**
- **Paperback publishers want bright ideas from booksellers for involving local children's groups, schools, etc.**

6 PUBLICITY: A PUBLISHER'S VIEW

By Eric Major
Publicity Director, Hodder & Stoughton

Do we, who are members of what is collectively called the book trade, make life difficult for ourselves when we come to consider publicity? My reaction to this question is to answer 'Yes we do', because we have traditional advantages denied other branches of industry or entertainment, but which we are slow to exploit.

After all, whether we are booksellers or publishers, we are all part of the communications industry or 'the media'. A long hard look at newspapers and magazines, radio and television and then at books will convince anyone that books are the most permanent aspect of the media, whose functions are: the recording of events, and the informing, entertaining and the educating of the people as a mass and as individuals.

One of the great appeals that books and authors have for journalists, feature editors, radio and television producers, is that, properly served up by the book trade publicist, there are news feature articles and personality profiles in abundance—enough to make those working in films or the theatre envious.

The main reason for this interaction between the communications media and the book is, as I stated earlier, because we are all involved in the same industry. One could argue that the book is in the modern sense the oldest part: Caxton and Gutenberg were printing and publishing books, not newspapers and magazines.

Who else but a publisher can contact influential decision-makers in the media? No other group has such an open door to the heart of the communications industry. A further reason for this is, I believe, the fact that we deal directly with the communications people ourselves. We seldom let the ubiquitous PR agents stand between ourselves, our authors and newspapers, magazines, radio and television. If, to many, what I have written may sound complacent and self-congratulatory, I remain unabashed.

The publicity manager

The activities of the publisher's publicity manager (I refuse to use the label public relations or press officer, which are misnomers in publishers' terms) directly assist the bookseller. It is his function to sell his company's wares which have been subscribed by the bookshop, and are the bookseller's livelihood. His energy and talent can often make the difference between that pile of twelve copies disappearing and a repeat order being obtained, or that pile of twelve copies gathering dust and being swept into the stockroom, later to be the subject of a request to the much-abused representatives to accept them back for credit.

The fruits of publishers' publicity efforts are often not recognised as such—the discussion of a book on a mid-afternoon television programme or radio programme; the reading or dramatisation of a book on radio; the author interview in a magazine or featuring in a woman's magazine. All these have often sold more books than reviews in the 'heavy' Sunday newspapers, however valuable or gratifying to the author's ego the latter may be, particularly if they are used on the dust cover of his next book!

But what is the publicist's link between the bookseller and the publisher? In almost every case where we consider 'free' publicity (do I hear a cry of 'Free for whom? ') the link is nearly always people. For it is people—their stories and their presence—that create comment, create news, create a crowd and create sales.

Signing sessions

The much abused signing session is the one link that springs immediately to mind. But a number of criteria must be studied before a firm decision is made to have best selling author X for a signing session—whether the pressure comes from the publisher, the author or the insistent requests of the bookseller. There can be nothing more embarrassing—and how we have all suffered— than a pile of books, the author sitting in front of them with his pen poised and not a buyer in sight. On these occasions it is also raining and half-day closing starts at 1 pm!

What are the essentials for a good signing session? Paramount is the co-operation of bookseller and publisher with agreement on date and times when there will be a high traffic into, or past, the shop or store. There must be heavy advance publicity: streamers, showcards, press advertising; publicity in the local newspapers; leaflets sent with accounts, and, if the subject of these attentions is a well-known personality, all publicity keyed in with photographs of the author.

The most important requirement is simplicity. Most of the initial arrangements may be organized by the representative; the publisher and bookseller may not actually meet until the day of the signing session. Therefore, all the design involved should be straightforward and unambiguous.

The display material should reach the bookseller at least three weeks before the function. Sufficient time should be allowed for the design, confirmation of copy with the bookseller, and the setting of the advertisements. These advertisements should appear the week before the event if 'weeklies' are used and from four to five days if the local evening newspaper is selected. Excellent results have been obtained when classified advertisements have been inserted in national dailies such as *The daily telegraph, The times* and the *Guardian.*

When the day of the signing session is reached, every effort must be made to ensure that there is free-moving traffic through the shop, that the author is met and that the table is in a well lit and spacious part of the shop.

Signing sessions can be successful if all the many details are worked out and if a close liaison is maintained between the bookseller and publisher. If they fail, signing sessions are the most wasteful form of time and money in which the book trade can participate. They are also the most distressing, certain to deflate even the most confident author.

Launching parties

Similar to signing sessions are launching parties for new books, and these have been profitably held in bookshops. As well as making a focus for the shop in the community, the launching party can, by careful use of invitations, introduce new customers. It can create effective publisher/bookseller co-operation and give the bookshop publicity in the press or on the local BBC or commercial radio station. John Prime in Kings Lynn has used this publicity very effectively.

The local newspaper

The local newspapers, daily and weekly, can be the bookseller's link with the public in his catchment area. Not only through advertising, but by contact with journalists in order to feed them stories of general interest about the business and about author visits to the shop, or schools, or exhibitions.

Remember, you don't have to go to the top to get some action; very often far better results can be obtained by taking a middle course. The editor is often too busy managing the newspaper to find the time to cover the story and event, and will inevitably delegate the job. It is far better to cultivate a journalist on the staff who has a knowledge of books and authors and who therefore has a vested interest in seeing that what he has researched and written is used.

The county magazines

A growing market for the county retailer should be the 'county magazine' which is an established part of the British magazine industry. These include such journals as *Essex countryside, East Anglian magazine, Lancashire life, Kent life, Warwickshire and Worcestershire magazine.* Once contact is made, stories about bygone local authors, literary societies and books of the past or rural interest can be fed to them and are invariably well received. The great advantage of these types of magazine is the high standard of illustration and the large amount of editorial space available. Some booksellers themselves (or alternatively librarians) review books of local interest in these journals.

Booksellers–use your local radio

It may be as well at this juncture to consider the growing role in the community of local radio as an important form of communication. Starting from a handful of local VHF stations, they have grown so that they now cover most of the main conurbations–often with two stations, BBC and Commercial in the same city. For instance, London has three stations while Birmingham, Newcastle, Manchester and Stoke, two stations each.

At the moment these stations, still in their development stage, would, I believe, welcome a visit from their local bookseller. They would be pleased to receive suggestions on how to cover books, as well as getting literary news in their locality in an entertaining and refreshing manner.

In recent months, W H Smith have been making efforts in this direction with contact being encouraged between their branch managers and local stations. Many of these stations are in the main streets or precincts of towns and cities. In fact Radio Medway's studios and offices are the old premises of the *Chatham news*; and Radio Piccadilly, Manchester, the commercial station, is situated in the new Piccadilly shopping Plaza; BBC Radio Leeds station is placed in the busy Merrion Centre. Such is the predominant pattern all round the country.

The number of people tuning into their local radio station grows month by month. The amount of advertising that the commercial stations carry is showing a healthy increase, as are the listeners' responses to phone-in programmes, record requests and competitions.

The literary brains trust and literary luncheon

Local radio has always been keenly interested in another form of publicity, one in which the author is at the centre of attraction: this is the Literary Brains Trust or the Literary Luncheon or Dinner. The great attraction for readers and bookshop customers is that they meet, talk to and hear, their favourite writers. The enormous coverage that these events receive–Christina Foyle's famous luncheons, those in Leeds where the sponsored literary luncheons of the Yorkshire Post are organised by the redoutable Richard Douro and the Bristol literary dinner run by a committee that includes Bristol solicitor Stephen Kew and bookseller John May of George's–indicate their popularity with the news media.

These well-organised functions with radio, press and television 'back-up' have, with the assistance of publishers, attracted leading political figures, international novelists, famous travellers and sportsmen, and the most recent phenomenon on bestseller lists, television and radio personalities.

I can see no reason why, with publisher's co-operation, such events cannot be organised throughout Britain to add to such events already arranged. The list is certainly wide; there are functions in Edinburgh at the time of the Festival; there is the informal atmosphere created by the Hebden Bridge Bookshop; the Strathmore Bookshop's popular luncheons at Compton, Berkshire; the Manchester booksellers' Library Theatre lunchtime lectures; the East Anglian Writers in Norwich, and a recent addition–the Birmingham Post's successful literary luncheon.

Yet despite this appearance of success, cities such as Liverpool, Nottingham, Glasgow, Newcastle, and Coventry; and Teesside, the South and the West of England, and Wales, are areas which still remain to be explored as literary luncheon possibilities. Good organisation, publicity, efficient catering facilities and enthusiastic co-operation between publishers and booksellers, could ensure an interested, book-buying audience.

To my mind, the best examples of such functions are those held in Bristol and Birmingham because of their lack of formality and friendly atmosphere. If I have any criticism it can be expressed as a plea to the Bristol organisers—will you *please* sell books.

It is a matter of regret that the justly famed W H Smith Literary Brains Trust is no more. Organised by Sydney Hyde and chaired by the perspicacious Lionel Hale, and on some occasions by the late Ivor Brown and Robert McDermott, they were a popular medium for bringing authors and readers, particularly school children, together—the literary scene was poorer at their passing.

Appeal to children

It is working for children, among the enthusiasm, fun and laughter that children generate, that brings to bookseller-and-publisher co-operation a completely new dimension. An example that immediately springs to mind is the Children's Book Show. After being established in London, this has now visited Glasgow, Manchester, Leeds and Bristol, being welcomed in each town by children, teachers and, particularly, by parents.

But it does not need a large or complicated organisation to bring publicity for children's books and authors to children and adults. The efforts of booksellers and publishers and authors such as Val Biro and his car Gumdrop, Michael Bond, the creator of Paddington, Robert Harbin and his origami puppets, H E Todd with his storytelling, Eric Thompson and his Magic Round about stories, have been consistently successful.

Another imaginative activity to encourage book-reading among children was the annual stand organised by W H Smith & Son at the Schoolboys' Exhibition, where each day celebrities of sport, TV, radio, stage and film and, of course, popular children's authors would sign books and autographs. Books were sold on the spot and in gratifying numbers. These exhibitions were, alas, discontinued.

How to organise visits

What are the essentials to organise an author-only event? Or the larger Book Weeks arranged successfully by paperback publishers such as Puffin or Knight? The first essential is time. Time to arrange publicity, posters and in-store displays, also, more important, to make sure the author is free. After all, most children's authors are also something else—teachers, actors, bank clerks, restaurant owners and sometimes even mothers! Six months to prepare is ideal, two months would be possible providing the author is available. Obviously, the author must be a good speaker and a good social mixer.

The best times are: half-term, summer holidays (in seaside towns), Christmas, Easter, Whitsun, and in selected areas, Saturday mornings.

It is essential that the publisher and bookseller meet to talk over all the problems and to decide who does what. These vital arrangements cannot be satisfactorily made by letters and telephone calls.

The author, or illustrator, must be capable of doing something in addition to sitting behind a desk signing copies of books. The ability to draw, tell stories or make things, to hold the children's attention, will make children want to possess, and parents wish to buy, the book that the author has been talking about. When a children's book promotion or book show is a success, there can be nothing in the book trade more satisfying.

Competitions

When supported by the local library, schools or Children's Book Group and involving the local bookshop, nothing creates more intense interest than a competition. Dougal posters, Collins Natural History essay and poster competition, the Magic Roundabout Easter bonnets, are a few of the competitions that have been successful for booksellers and publishers. Carefully planned, with well-known judges and with prizes not only for the winner but also for the pupil's school ensures co-operation for the future.

The opening day of the Book Show, or the author's visit, is an ideal time to make the presentation of prizes to winners of any competition that has been organised: local press and radio, and even the area BBC or independent television station may be interested in the author's visit, profiles of the author in the local paper, and advertising, can help to guarantee a crowd when the author arrives.

One day there may be a 'Book Promotion Rent-a-Crowd', but until then a good gathering from schools, youth organisations and book groups can be found to greet the author on his arrival. Background music before and after the author's talk or signing session helps to relax the audience and create a happy atmosphere. Then there are giveaways to consider–badges, balloons,–something for the children to take away with them.

As any parent or teacher knows, children can be tiring. Give the author rest-breaks if the show goes on for several hours; a glass of water on the table and someone always in attendance. Afterwards, get him to sign some copies of the books for the children who have been unable to get to the show. And do then please write and thank the author–these letters mean so much and make him look forward with pleasure to the next time.

Conclusion

In all publicity, whatever is involved, the one important element is enthusiasm: a little enthusiasm goes a long way. And we need more of it in the book trade.

All of us, in bookselling and publishing, have to compete against more highly organised industries using skilled advertising agencies and sophisticated marketing techniques. Yet we have on our side the communications media who look upon us as their allies–but it is up to us to maintain our links with them. It is not their role constantly to harry us for information and authors and ideas.

We have to be more forthcoming. In the past we have been prone to secrecy, keeping the good ideas about books to ourselves. The media will help us–if we help them. It is a two-way traffic.

The publisher is frequently the prime mover, but he is very ready to respond to any initiative from the bookseller and to welcome his suggestions, enthusiasm and co-operation. Often this can come from young assistants and this is particularly to be welcomed.

KEYNOTES

- Publishers have an open door to the media.
- Publishers' publicity people usually deal directly with the media, not through PR agents as most other trades and professions.
- Publicity managers secure the reading on radio, the interview on TV, the article in the newspaper or magazine, all of which contribute positively to sales.
- People are news.
- Author signing sessions must be carefully planned by publisher and bookseller alike. Only-used traffic areas should be considered. The publisher's representative is almost always a key figure.
- Advertising must be carefully prepared in advance.
- Publisher launching parties held in bookshops make excellent publicity for the shop.
- Establish a friendly relationship with a journalist on the local paper who really cares about books.
- Don't overlook county magazines. Booksellers are often asked to review books for them.
- Local radio stations are frequently short of news items.
- Literary lunches and dinners are both good in themselves and of strong interest to local radio stations too.
- If you're planning an exhibition or other event, make sure you allow sufficient preparatory time. Big ones may need a year or more to organise in every detail.
- When an event is a joint effort, publisher and bookseller must meet in advance, not just write letters or telephone.
- Competitions are a sure way of arousing interest in books.
- Don't forget that children can be tiring: give your author rest periods. And after it is all over, don't forget to write and say thank you.

7 DISPLAY

This chapter deals with the theory of bookshop display and with the methods and materials which are available to make that theory a reality.

The changes in retailing patterns–most clearly seen in the self-service supermarkets–are surveyed, and their impact on book merchandising is discussed. There are also sections on shopfitting and on the lighting of bookshops.

PRINCIPLES AND PRACTICE

by Peter Giddy, Managing Director, Hatchards

The very use of the word 'display' is, to my mind, self-defeating; it suggests rigidity and a sense of permanence that inhibits the customer and stops him from handling the books with which you are trying to tempt him.

In any bookshop, half the battle is won when a shopper picks up the books on show. If, by the formality of the display, he feels the slightest bit deterred, you will lose him. It must be remembered that very few people need to enter a bookshop, and if they do feel a need then we, as booksellers, should encourage them by being as friendly and open as possible. I would like to think that the days when people visited a bookshop as if they were entering a mysterious shrine to some frightening gods, are over.

These few remarks do not mean that there is no need for care in showing your stocks, but there is great need to do it in ways that tempt your customers. Within any shop there are those places where display is important, and I propose to deal with them in the order that the customer sees them.

Windows

It probably seems a stupid remark, but these are vital to your prosperity. It is only by lively and attractive shows in your windows that you can catch the interest of a passer by who doesn't know anything about current books. All windows need to be brightly and attractively lit. If you have old fashioned lighting equipment, look into the possibility of using the track system which enables you to put spot-lights in positions that help you to make the most of your set-pieces. It is not expensive, and the difference it can make is spectacular.

Unless you are doing 'solo windows', try and put in as many *related* titles as possible, but not just one copy of each. Try to break up the regularity by standing books upon one another, building up towers of the same size books but of different titles. Sometimes it pays to make it a little difficult to read a title; it is amazing how a person craning his neck can soon attract a little crowd.

If you are treating a subject, say gardening, horse-riding, clocks or anything else, try and get your local fellow tradesmen to help. Borrow some of their stock, and give them credit in your window. They will normally respond to this kind of approach and even reciprocate by showing some of your books in their special displays. My experience has proved the value of this over and over again.

Whilst on this subject, it pays to get in touch with societies catering for local or special interests. I am thinking in particular of the way that many building societies set up displays that have absolutely no relation to their business, but use their windows simply to promote feeling of relationship within a community. Many local societies will be only too willing to help, and some of their material is spectacular.

If you possibly can–get animation into the window–it is a splendid crowd-stopper. Use anything that is relevant and try to be amusing if the subject can be treated in that way.

If you are unfortunate enough only to have a window fitted with sloping back shelves for display, most of the previous suggestions are impracticable. In this case, you must remember that it is important to keep the window looking as fresh and clean as possible. A depressing, ill-arranged window suggests the shop is the same, so dusty, dirty, scruffy marked copies, which are a disgrace to your shop, should be banned from windows in all cases.

The previous paragraph leads to the final point about windows: try to make sure that anyone who looks into your window can also look through into your shop. Do away with backs or dusty curtains, or anything that impedes a view through. Let those outside know that it is even better inside.

Shop tables and special displays

The tables we all use are a particular problem. Their main purpose is to carry the stocks that we wish our customers to buy; it is not their job to be regulated and so tidy that the customer is frightened off. Any table display (for want of a better word) that is formal, fails utterly in its purpose. A good idea, psychologically, is to have piles of books as large as possible, but within easy reach of the customers' hands. Another good idea is to have two piles of the same book–one containing say eight copies, and the other one or two. This suggests that that particular book is going down at a fast rate, and we all know the power of suggestion.

If you do elaborate displays on special stands or tables, it is important also to have copies that your customers can handle without fear of being buried under your showpiece should they touch a book. Avoid stacking odd copies on their fore-edges so that only the spine is showing. The correct place for these singles and doubles is on the shelves.

Try to feature the books in your window displays fairly close to the door. It doesn't matter if they are usually kept in another part of the shop; the important thing is to get the book into your customer's hand as quickly as possible. If this is not possible, make sure that the department concerned has the book well to the fore, so that your customer can get to them without asking again. If you are displaying a wide selection of your stock in the window, try to have a typed list available so that the customer who asks for a particular book can be sent immediately to the correct place in your shop. It is infuriating for them to have to come in and then find that they have got to ask and ask and go from one assistant to another.

If possible try to use tables of different shapes. It is feasible with small square tables to buy circular tops for them, cut from reasonably strong plyboard, and to put these on top. It is interesting and enlightening to see how people will move round and around a circular table, whilst they are inclined to stand, four-square, to the normal oblong one.

Shelving and general stock

The use of shelves for display is seriously limited, but it should be borne in mind that shelves that are between 2 ft 6 in and 5 ft 6 in high are the easiest for the customers to select from. Because of this, it pays to put your best shelf-lines into these shelves and to give a face-forward display as much as possible. Shelves below and above this height can be kept in good order, but you will find that you will have to take these books from them for your customer. Much more self-service is possible from those of the ideal height.

An important point about shelf stock is that it should be arranged in the most rational way possible–fiction, certainly, in alphabetical order; but most other categories should be arranged under subject, rather than under author or publisher. If you are asked for a Greek cookery book, for example, it is no good knowing there are three in your stock if you have got to remember the authors. It is much easier to point straightaway to the three of them together so that your customer can then make his own choice, only offering further assistance if he should ask for it. This, of course, also helps your staff if someone has to help in a strange department through sickness or holidays.

One neglected area for display is stockrooms. It is important, within stockrooms, that books are kept as logically as possible. If you run a shop where representatives call frequently, it is an advantage to keep your stock both in subject and publisher order. If you have to do your own stock re-ordering, it is vital that anyone sent to the stockroom be able to survey the stock at a glance, rather than having to locate it, or scrub through various parcels which are half-opened and untidy.

Conclusion

Display, to my mind, is much more of a science than an art. Its sole purpose is to enable you to sell your goods to your customers as quickly and efficiently as possible. It should not be designed just to make the shop look tidy or pretty; it is there solely to tempt would-be purchasers.

The word 'display', as I wrote in my introduction, has unfortunate connotations of rigidity and fixed, untouchable exhibits–but I cannot think of a better word.

However, it is the *approach* to display that matters, and the ringing of the cash register will tell us if our approach is the right one.

No 1: Author H E Todd ('Toddy') telling a story in Woolworths, Bournemouth.

No. 2: TV personality Eric Thompson and 'Dougal' with children from the local primary school after a storytelling session at the Children's Book Centre in west London.

No 5: One of the regular press advertisements for Book Tokens, in this case showing young people of various ages enjoying books.

No 4: The K-5 system of paperback display racking, which can be tailored to fit almost any premises.

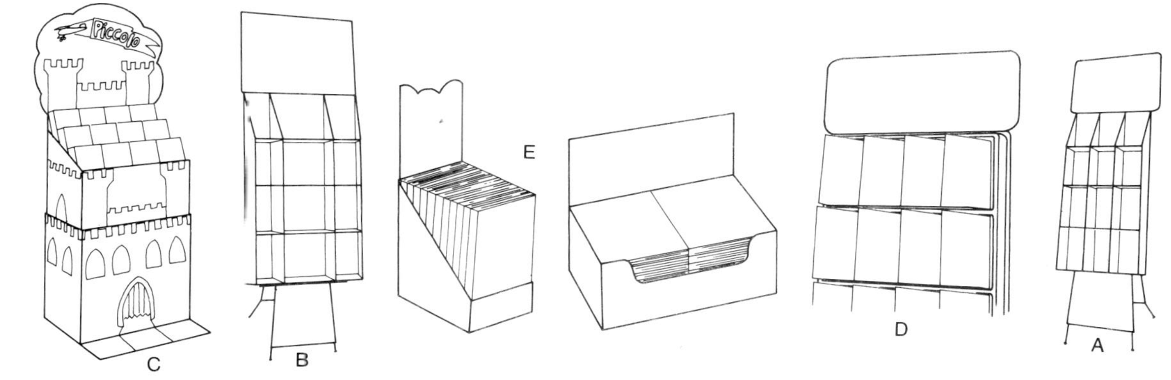

No 5: Types of 'bin' for paperback display. A is a standard 12-pocket bin on a wire base. B is a double-format type allowing upright and landscape display. C is a special novelty 'haunted castle' bin from Pan Books. D is a semi-permanent plastic bin for bigger promotions. E shows (left) the shoe-box display pack, and (right) the flat pack with fold-up header.

Nos 6 & 7: Two competition displays in Newcastle-upon-Tyne in 1974; Thorne's Students Bookshop's winning entry, and a display at the Hancock Museum.

GARDENING, FLOWERS
NEW NATURALIST, FIELD & POCKET GUIDES
The New Naturalist Library

No 8: (a) Wall- or ceiling-mounted reflector spotlamp; (b) Ceiling-mounted metal cylinder.

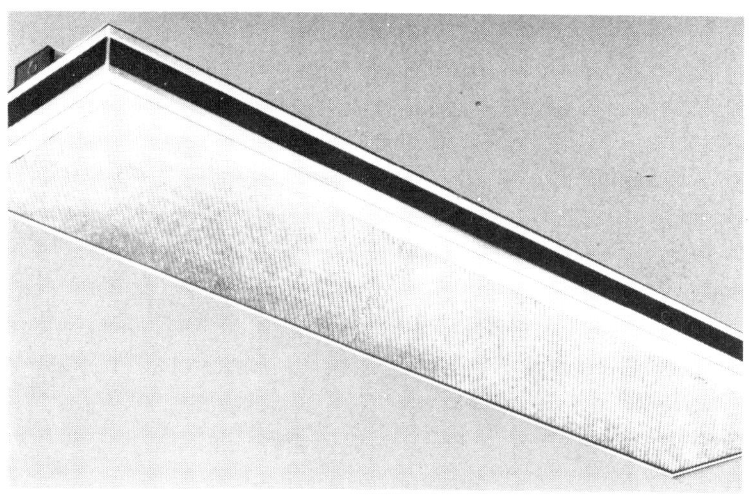

No 9: Two different types of fluorescent tube fittings.

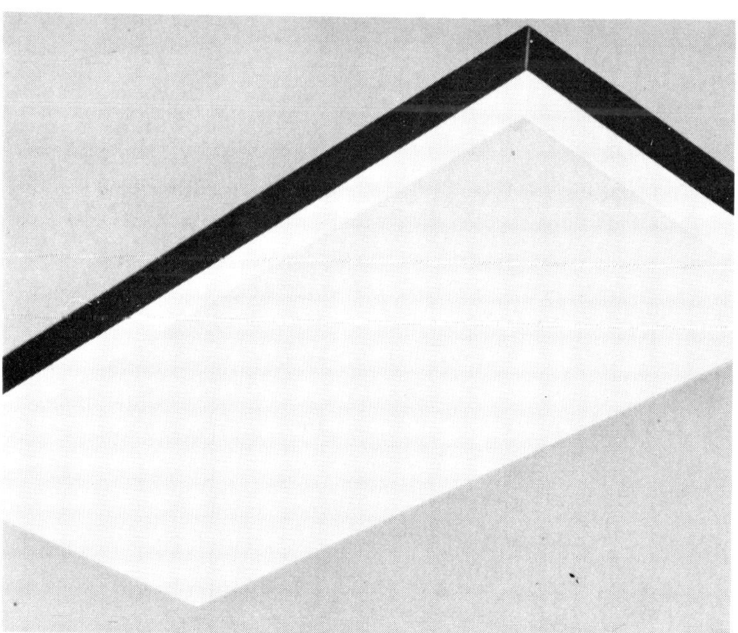

Books
Books

Nos 10 & 11: Cool, elegant and effective layout and lighting at W H Smith & Son Ltd's Woolwich shop, southeast London.

VISER OG SANGER
BIOGRAFIER
FRILUFTSLIV
ROMANER
LYRIKK
ROMANER

Nos 12 & 13: Two views of the interior of F Beyer Bokhandel in Bergen, Norway's oldest bookshop, dating from 1771. The Swedish-made shelving gives excellent display plus economy of space.

No 14: The W P van Stockum bookshop in the Hague, Holland, originally founded in 1836, and now part of the Elsevier chain of bookshops.

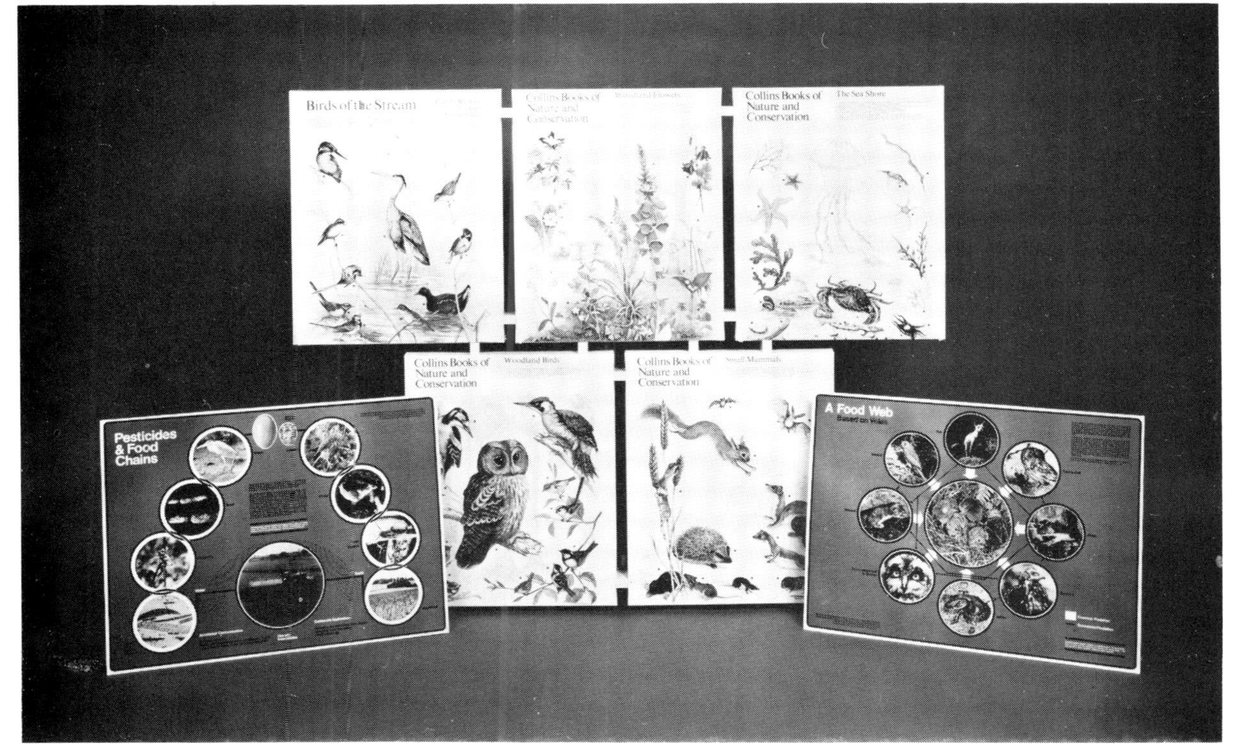

No 15: Collins' wall-charts and posters for schools.

No 16: The use of modular cubes in a typical window display.

BOOK MERCHANDISING

by J N B Barden, W H Smith & Son Ltd

Many factors contribute to the success of a bookshop, and they can be briefly described as follows:

Careful selection of merchandise
Effective control of stock levels
Efficient and practical clerical systems
An effective well-trained staff
Effective presentation and display of merchandise.

It is the last mentioned of these factors–effective presentation and display of merchandise–which we will consider here in more detail.

The techniques to be employed for merchandising and displaying books can be examined under various headings. It must be stressed however, that a degree of flexibility must be built in, whereby these techniques can be adapted or modified to suit the prevailing physical limitations in any given bookshop.

Vertical merchandising

Generally speaking, books displayed on shelves can be presented in a horizontal dressing or a vertical dressing. Extensive research has shown that the vertical arrangement is more effective and leads to a higher incidence of impulse sales.

Let us first consider what we mean by 'Vertical Merchandise'. It is simply a vertical arrangement of related titles dressed over the modular size of fittings used in the shop. (The modular size will alter from shop to shop, but practical experience has shown that the maximum modular size should be no more than 4 ft.) This arrangement of merchandise has distinct advantages that may be summarised as follows:

a A vertical block of books creates visual impact, thus enabling the customer to identify each classified section.

b This arrangement maximises the customer's choice when standing in front of fittings.

c When viewed from a distance, all merchandise classification can be seen at one level.

d It is an aid to better related displays, both within a department and between adjoining departments.

e It is an aid to self-selection; the classifications assisting the customers to make their purchases.

The method for adjoining a vertical arrangement of merchandise is quite simple. The merchandise is dressed from the left-hand side of the top shelf down to the right-hand side of the bottom shelf, and as one module is completed the next is started.

Classification

The integral part of book merchandising is display classification, and a system should be developed whereby each vertical module can be classified by using Header Cards or other sign boards. The range of classification headings will be determined by the range of merchandise stocked in any given bookshop, but it is important to remember that the headings should be generic rather than specific. (In larger shops it is possible, of course, to classify generically and sub-divide using more specific titles.)

It is important to resist the temptation to classify by publisher rather than subject. A customer will expect to find any given title under its appropriate subject and not under the name of the publisher.

The overall layout and classification of the shop should follow a logical sequence; in other words, careful consideration should be given to the location of General books non-fiction, General books fiction, Children's books, and Paperbacks. Classification within each department should also follow a logical sequence, so that related sections are located adjacent to one another.

General notes on presentation

The following points should always be kept in mind when displaying merchandise:

a All merchandise must be classified and the Header Cards must be clearly visible.

b All merchandise must be clearly visible and easily accessible.

c Wherever possible, merchandise must be displayed face-on and in the maximum quantities.

d Displays of merchandise should be bold, simple and eye-catching.

e When dressing out, the shelves should be continually adjusted to make the most economical use of space.

f Merchandise should be displayed in bulk, and one item should not be obscured by another item.

g Routine cleaning and dusting, of both fittings and merchandise, is essential if displays are to be maintained in mint condition.

h Special techniques should be employed for paperbacks because all titles are of a similar size and format. If possible, the shelves between adjoining classifications should be staggered slightly so that the entire department is visually classified.

Summary

The above notes explain the general principles to be adopted when displaying books. Experience will determine the more detailed techniques to be used with particular types of books such as maps, guides and the children's flat books. Whilst practical adaptation of these principles will be inevitable in many situations, the overall guide lines should be adhered to at all times.

FITTINGS

by Donald Simm, Chief Architect, W H Smith & Son Ltd

Over the past thirty years, three basic types of general display systems have been used, all of which present a similar image while using materials that are very different.

The first shopfitting system was basically all constructed of timber. This meant that each shop had a custom-built interior. A shopfitter would be given the details of each individual shop, that is, the physical characteristics. He would then manufacture the required fittings, transport them to the site and install, which would also involve considerable joinery work on site.

Modular systems

The second method was the incorporation of a modular shopfitting system. This was the bringing together of both timber and metal, via the shopfitter's work, and a shopfitting display system manufactured by others. The system generally introduced was a 2 ft 6 in module, comprising vertical metal columns at 2 ft 6 in centres, fixed to the wall or free-standing, with timber infill panels between these columns. To this wall lining would be attached 5 ft long timber or glass shelves covering two modules, which were supported from the channel on brackets. These shelves and brackets were adjustable vertically, but it was not possible to angle them up or down as the brackets were fixed horizontally. This meant that some shelves had to be custom made in timber and fitted to suit.

The metre module

The third system, which in fact is being used to this present day, is a 2 ft or 1 metre module, all metal equipment, wherein all components are standard and supplied by a shop display equipment manufacturer. They are usually installed on site by a shopfitter.

It is encumbent upon the shopfitter to install various detailed finishes to the above-mentioned, all-metal perimeter lining system. This modular metal display equipment system is fully adjustable; and the standard range of components available is so comprehensive that virtually any merchandise can be displayed using standard components.

Advantages

There are several advantages with the later systems over the first because:

1 The speed of manufacture and erection is increased considerably.

2 Control of cost in these days of inflation.

3 Virtually complete versatility of display technique.

4 Using a standard system means that every shop is, and looks, very similar, and therefore it is possible to create a nationwide image.

5 Satisfactory relationships with local authorities' regulations, which are becoming more stringent every day.

More on display

Because of contemporary display techniques and retailing patterns, the system now evolved concentrates the merchandise within easy reach of the customer. Linked with the new methods of self-service and supermarket-type trading, this has meant that much more merchandise can be on display, whereas previously certain quantities of merchandise were in fact not available to the public. These were stored in cupboards or drawers, which proved to be expensive and is now unnecessary. The modular shopfitting systems are applicable equally to either wall or island fittings.

The latest modular display systems now in use, enabling departmental ranges to be vertically merchandised, simply means that any one item of merchandise can be displayed with one vertical module, and therefore the complete range is within the customers' eyeline. Previously, similar merchandise would have been displayed horizontally, which proved to be unsatisfactory because it offered little control. This system offers as many advantages to the staff working in the shop as it does to the customers, which can only help the overall concept to be satisfactory from all aspects.

Costs

As a guide to costs, the situation in June 1975 is £27 per foot run of fitting or £22 per square foot of sales area. It must be appreciated, however, that there are many reasons why costs can vary from guide figures.

LIGHTING FOR BOOKSHOPS

by W K Lumsden, Chief Lighting Engineer, Thorn Lighting Ltd

Vision

The human eye is able to see well in very different lighting conditions– from moonlight to mid-day sunlight– but it functions most effectively, however, in less extreme conditions over a limited range of brightnesses. Visual disability, physical discomfort and muscular fatigue can result if the eye is presented at any one time with objects or lamps having wide differences in brightness.

At rest the eye is focused at infinity and it automatically exerts muscular effort to focus on near objects, as when reading. In any situation where the eye is required constantly to re-focus on near and distant objects, it is not uncommon to find complaints of 'eye-strain'. In many cases this is simply fatigue of the focusing muscles.

Quantity of light

All light–natural and artificial– is a form of electro-magnetic radiation that the eye is tuned to receive similarly to the way in which a radio receiver is tuned to receive a particular station. Differences between light sources are in the colour, the brightness and the degrees of diffusion, not in the basic nature of light.

Light is a flow of energy which continues as long as the source is switched on; and in practical installations, part of the energy is absorbed as heat by the room surface–the darker the colour the more light is absorbed. The proportion not absorbed produces a value of illumination on objects and surfaces in the room which can be measured by a light-meter. Usually a lighting design starts with the specification of the illumination value needed, and the lighting engineer then calculates the number of lamps needed to produce that value.

The Illuminating Engineering Society of Great Britain publishes a *Code* giving guidance on values of illumination needed for different types of interiors and for different jobs. These values are quoted in units of 'lux', which is the amount of light flux in lumens, incident on one square metre. For example–a 100 watt lamp emits about 1200 lumens, and if all this light could be directed on to a surface of 4 square metres, the illumination on the surface would be:

$$\frac{1200}{4} = 300 \text{ lux (lumens per square metre)}$$

Lighting from artificial sources in buildings varies from 1000 lux in modern offices to 150 lux in corridors.

The illumination in bookshops needs to be specified carefully as there are two distinct functions for the lighting. One is the lighting of book titles in vertical shelves and a typical value would be 150 lux on the back of the books; the other is the lighting for *reading* the books which would generally be held horizontally, and this should be around 300 lux. The type of shop, trading competition in the locality, the type of books sold and the type of readers could all affect the choice of illumination; but in general, the values quoted should be regarded as the lowest for comfortable seeing. It should be noted that the Shops & Offices Act requires lighting to be sufficient and suitable.

Quality of light

It would be possible to produce 300 lux on books using either a bare 100 watt lamp, 3 in away from the book, or by a 150 watt spotlight 20 ft away. In the case where the source is right in the field of view, its high brightness will cause the eye to adapt to see best at that brightness, and it will not see so well the lower brightness of the book. This is called glare, and glare reduces the effective value of illumination on a task and can, in cases such as this, be very uncomfortable. Glare can be caused by any extreme brightness contrasts in the field of view, and the higher brightness can be from a lamp, a window, or the reflected image in a polished surface.

The quality of the lighting in the sense of the impression made on users of a room depends to an extent on the colour appearance of the surfaces and objects, and these can vary considerably depending on the light source selected. The lamp should be chosen to show colours as the designer wishes, and considerable assistance is given in the IES Code on this point.

Incandescent lamps

This type of lamp combines low initial cost with good colour rendering, but has the disadvantages of a short lamp life–1000 hours nominal, and low efficiency. The lamp is susceptible to relatively small changes in applied voltages, for instance a 10 per cent increase in the rated voltage increases light output by nearly half, but reduces life to about a quarter of the nominal. The low efficiency of this lamp makes it very expensive to use for high illumination values over large areas; but, in spotlight form, it is ideal for producing high illumination values on displays.

Reflector spotlamps

These are tungsten filaments enclosed in a pressed-glass bulb, the back of which is parabolic in cross-section and usually internally silvered. The filament is mounted at the focus of the parabola, and the front glass can incorporate lenses to control the beam width. These lamps produce a high illumination over a small area; a typical distribution would be a spot of 3 ft diameter from 10 ft away, but there are many different light distributions available.

Fluorescent tubes

These have the advantages of very high efficiencies and exceptionally long life (7500 hours) and are used extensively for general lighting. A wide range of different 'Whites' is available, varying from very cold 'Northlight' to very warm de luxe 'Warm White'.

Fluorescent tubes need control gear to operate them, which increases the capital cost compared with incandescent lighting; but this is recovered fairly quickly by the saving in running costs due to the higher efficiency of the lamp.

Colour corrected mercury lamps (MBF)

This lamp has size and shape similar to incandescent lamps, but in colour and operation it is similar to fluorescent tubes. Modern versions are very efficient, with good colour rendering properties, and can be used for offices and shops. Installation design needs more careful attention, and a lighting engineer should be consulted. Control gear is needed for these lamps.

Lighting fittings

The function of a fitting is to hold the lamp, connect it to an electrical supply, and control the distribution of light. Fittings vary considerably in their efficiency in letting light out, and in the way they control distribution. The performance of different fittings can, however, be easily compared by first-hand inspection.

Light output ratio

Usually expressed as percentage and is the proportion of lamp flux that leaves the fitting, the remainder being absorbed as heat within the fitting. This figure has a considerable bearing on the costs of lighting, and all other factors being equal the fitting with the highest light output ratio should be selected.

British zonal classification

Expressed as a single number usually between one and seven, and describes the light distribution of the fitting downwards. Number one is a very narrow distribution and number seven is very broad.

The BZ classification should be chosen to give the distribution required. BZ1 provides mainly down lighting for reading, but does not illuminate the shelves; so additional lighting is needed from spotlights. With this scheme the ceiling, the fittings and the walls would appear dark, and light would be concentrated on the books. BZ7 provides light for reading and for the bookshelves– no supplementary lighting is needed. The room in this case would be generally bright and would give a completely different impression.

Flux fraction

Shown as percentage of the light from the fitting emitted up and down. This factor tells you whether or not your ceiling will be illuminated, and from that what the general appearance of your shop will be.

Installation and design

'General lighting' is the term used to describe the conventional system which uses fluorescent discharge or incandescent fittings, spaced regularly across the ceiling, to give a designed average value of illumination. Occasionally, where more effective lighting is needed on the bookshelves, a system of local lighting is used to supplement the illumination produced by the overhead system.

Lighting for the shelves and for reading could be provided from lighting fittings fixed to the shelves. This is a particularly useful technique for high ceilinged shops.

In planning the lighting, some thought should be given to the switching to ensure the safety and convenience of customers, and for security. In addition, a suitable switching system should allow some lights, in appropriate positions, to be switched on at night to advertise the shop.

Flexibility in the use of lighting can often be provided by the use of Trak systems of lighting which carry current to each fitting, and allow individual switching.

There is no doubt that appropriate lighting will contribute considerably to the impression in a customer's mind of the shop and the quality of merchandise. Careful thought should be given to all aspects of lighting and the effect of these on the lighted environment.

Many manufacturers and contractors, including the Electricity Boards, are glad to give advice on the proper use of lighting equipment, and in the case of large shops, they will often produce detailed drawings and specifications.

KEYNOTES

- **Windows must be brightly lit.**
- **Use related titles in window displays.**
- **Borrow specialist items from other local traders and credit the loan in your display.**

- Use animation in the window whenever possible.
- Make sure people can see into the shop so avoid high-backed window displays.
- Arrange display tables fairly casually so the customer won't be afraid of disturbing the display when he picks up a book.
- Don't squeeze in odd copies on their fore-edges: display copies should be flat, face up.
- Books in the window should be featured near the door inside the shop.
- Circular display tables encourage people to move round them.
- Have as much face forward display on shelves as you can manage.
- Arrange books in the stockroom logically for quick and easy reference to them.
- Shelve related titles vertically: it's easier for the customer to identify what he wants.
- Classify by subject and have clear, general header cards to announce the subjects.
- Always adjust shelves to make the most economical use of space.
- Books, shelves and displays must be frequently cleaned and dusted.
- Metal modular shelving has many advantages, apart from speed of shopfitting, over other types.
- Fluorescent lighting costs more to install but much less to run than ordinary lighting.

8 ADVERTISING

This chapter opens with a detailed guide on how to use the newspaper press for advertising, including the preparation of material, layout and insertion.

The second part deals with the problems of direct mail bookselling. Finally, there is a section on catalogues–publishers' and booksellers' catalogues, and the pervasive, subject and topic catalogues produced by Book Promotion Services.

PRESS ADVERTISING

by Sydney T Hyde

The subject of press advertising for bookshops is a contentious one and is very frequently influenced by factors that have more to do with implied threats than with advertising values. When a bookseller says that he spends £500 per annum on advertising, he frequently means that an expenditure of £500 has been charged to advertising, which can be a very different matter.

His true advertising expenditure may well be no more than half this amount. The other half has been extracted from him through his own generosity towards local activities, or by the threat of lost business from local institutions whose custom is regarded as being dependent upon his support to the advertising pages of bulletins, news letters, magazines etc, that have for him no true advertising value.

What he does about them must be a matter for his own judgement: nobody can lay down rules for him to follow; for only he knows how much substance there is in the implied threats and his own fears. Only he knows the risks because personalities are involved. But don't let him confuse this with press advertising.

Thus here we leave out of account, though they often comprise a large proportion of advertising expenditure, the parish magazines, the various programmes of the local drama, opera and music groups, parents association magazines and all the publications that fall into these and similar categories.

Your local newspaper

What about the local newspaper? Of course, to most booksellers who are not indulging in mail order, this is what press advertising is about. There are two main aspects to consider. The first is consideration of its value in terms of cementing of good relations with the paper which, broadly, amounts to public relations.

Looked at from a purely commercial point of view, the local press has a good claim to favourable consideration. At the same time, some qualification is necessary. In this connection the factors are, of course, the nature of the area, the quality of the newspaper, geographical considerations, readership in terms of circulation and quality of circulation.

It would be difficult to justify, for booksellers, frequent and regular advertising in the local paper, however good the quality of the newspaper. Only products or services essential to the family's health and feeding, or products in constant use in the home, where sales are repetitive and brands varied, can justify such expenditure; and ours is not such a product.

On the other hand, for this very reason, our shops are not well used in general and consequently become too frequently overlooked. So that when the book is needed, many people, as we know all too well, cannot easily call to mind where to get it. It is good, therefore, for reminders to appear from time to time and at appropriate times.

However, a flabby 'Visit your local bookshop' is not the way to do it. Tie the advertisement to something topical or specific, such as Christmas, back to school, the gardening season, home decoration; to an outstanding current subject of discussion, or to a new book or series of widespread interest. Make use, from time to time, of the Book Tokens offer to meet half the cost of local advertising, and use blocks supplied by them; thus saving yourself the trouble of preparing the advertisement. Or, again, take advantage of a publisher's offer to share the cost of an advertisement when he is launching a big book or series. This has been covered in other chapters.

If one secures useful free publicity in the local paper in the form of coverage for authors' visits, special campaigns, special displays, reviews of outstanding books etc, it is sensible and fair to offer some return in advertising support from time to time. Neither should we be too hasty to call this a form of blackmail. The plain fact is that the more publicity a bookshop can get in the form of free publicity, which is of more value generally than paid advertising, the better for the bookshop. The newspaper relies on advertising revenue for survival and it is in the interest of the bookshop that it should survive, and if it can flourish, then better still.

First considerations

If you are going to advertise, you must decide therefore on certain points, although not necessarily in this order: a) How much are you prepared to spend? b) How much space can you buy for the proposed expenditure? c) What are you going to advertise? d) How to go about it?

Events will decide the order. Having decided upon a, b, c, what now? It is often the question of 'how to go about it' that is the off-putting factor and provides the excuse for doing nothing. It need not. You can make it as complicated or as simple for yourself as you wish.

How to set about advertising

Follow certain basic principles. Keep copy and lay-out simple. Don't spend sleepless nights striving to be clever and to out-do Schweppes, or BP, or Heinz in originality. It is neither necessary nor appropriate. Their problems are very different from yours and often, in national advertising, it is a matter of the creative teams of one agency competing against another, rather than total concern with the product.

You have little money to spend, so let common sense be the guide. Remember that your local newspaper is pretty crowded with advertisements, so go for boldness and try to buy a position that adjoins editorial matter, or as near the top of a right hand page as you can.

Be bold in the use of borders, and in the type and lay-out you use—and don't be afraid of white space. Because the space is costing you £15, don't fill every square centimetre! You want the advertisement to be seen and to compete with its neighbouring advertisements on the same page—advertisements that will often be bigger than yours. The temptation to crowd your little four-inch double column ad with as many titles or as much wording (copy) as possible, in the belief that you are getting maximum value for money, is to be resisted. Remember that first and foremost your advertisement must command attention and on a crowded page white space is not wasted space.

You may say that you know nothing about type faces and lay-out. Don't let that deter you; you don't have to know the name of a single type face, nor have you to be able to draw. There is danger in conceit arising from ignorance. So many won't admit it and kid themselves that they are equipped to produce original lay-outs.

Advertising is too often regarded as a pleasant and harmless diversion from one's daily chores and a way of ridding oneself of inhibitions. So, they say to themselves, let us put it all askew (as if that was an original thought), let us show them! Or let us use some awful shadow type that nobody in his senses uses these days, because you can't read it easily anyway. Above all, don't, may I beg of you, give the job to your young daughter to play with to keep her amused when she has finished her homework. If this sounds facetious, let me assure you that it is not uncommon in any trade. Advertising is too often regarded as everybody's plaything.

Wording on 'copy'

Let the copy be direct, informative and bright. It must briefly show good cause why the book should be bought. It may be a worthwhile book because of its information for the professional or the layman. Maybe the quality of the writing, or the author's reputation is most important. On the other hand, you may wish to stress the physical make-up and production of the book. Whichever aspects are selected, some good crisp indication of the merits of the book should be stated.

The lay-out of your advertisement

Having decided what you are to advertise, what you wish to say about it, and any other information to be included, you can do the lay-out yourself or ask the newspaper to do it for you; they will be happy to do it. It is not necessary to be a typographer in order to do it yourself. It can be as simple as that shown in the illustration.

Note how roughly your requirements are indicated. The compositor can be relied upon to interpret them and use the most suitable type, given some indication of what you have in mind. Do not forget, however, that most

A when he will sign copies of his books and, in particular, his new book "Doctor, Doctor"

B PILGRIM'S BOOKSHOP, 14 GREEN STREET, CARDIFF Tel. CARDIFF, 6060603

PRINTER: Please set bold, and use bold, medium and light rules as indicated on layout.

The layout can be as simple and uncomplicated as this!

local newspapers have not the means of producing, from their own resources, advertisements to the standard of those in national newspapers and magazines. Don't be bashful about cutting out an advertisement from your local paper and telling them that you want your advertisement to look like that. This can be a satisfactory, direct approach to the problem. If you happen to know something about type, by all means specify the type you prefer, but do be prepared to compromise because it may well be that the local newspaper has not got exactly what you want.

When should the bookshop advertise?

When is it reasonable to advertise a bookshop locally? At Christmas time, obviously, when you are in competition with almost every other trader and anxious to get home the message of books as Christmas presents–and that it is your shop from which they should be bought. When the schools, evening institutes, technical colleges, and art schools go back from vacation is a good time. Special occasions, as discussed elsewhere in this book, such as author's visits (in which case you would normally be working with the publisher who will doubtless do all the work for you, and, with luck, pay up as well).

Special displays and campaigns when, again, you may be working with a single publisher, or making your own selection of books from a number of publishers. Gardening books, do-it-yourself books, holiday guides, motoring books, are obvious possibilities. Then, of course, there are at times special local events attracting considerable interest and publicity that may well be used for special displays in the bookshop and modest advertising.

The cost

Local press advertising is not going to cost you a fortune. It can be expensive though if you are situated in the central areas of a large town where the newspaper has a large circulation because, naturally enough, advertising rates are geared to circulation.

The cost of one single column inch can vary from as little as 50 pence to as much as 770 pence. As a rough average one could think in terms of 85 pence perhaps. So the average cost of an advertisement measuring four inches deep across two columns would be £6.80; but, according to your location, may be as little as £4.40, or as much as £61 in a large city paper.

However, most large towns have suburban papers or groups of suburban papers and these are the ones you should, of course, use if you are outside the city area; otherwise you are paying for a great deal of wasted circulation.

Some advertising terms

Here are some advertising terms that you, the bookseller, may encounter when telephoning your newspaper to book the space. You may be asked if you want 'Classified or display'. Classified advertisements are those sold by the line, as for instance, the usual advertisements for flats, houses, second-hand household equipment, cars, and so on. Display advertisements are sold by the page, half page, column or inch. You will need the display department.

You may be asked if your advertisement is to be 'trade set' or 'paper set'. This means, is the advertisement to be set by a printer and supplied in block form, or is it to be set by the newspaper itself? Here you may also encounter the expression 'pub set' or 'publisher set'—this means the same thing. Yours will be paper, or pub, set. (Not to be confused with the book publisher.)

You may be asked about your 'copy', which means the wording of your advertisement. Are you using 'half-tone' or 'line'—are you using illustrations and if so, will you be reproducing from a photograph or just a simple black and white sketch? If it is a photograph or an illustration with tones, it will be a half-tone block that has to be made. If it is a simple drawing, such as a cartoon or sketch, then a line block is required. But you will probably want neither.

Don't be too disconcerted if they convert your inches into centimetres. Some do this already and maybe you do. We all have to get accustomed to this!

DIRECT MAIL BOOKSELLING: GOLDMINE OR SWAMP?

by Gerald Bartlett, Managing Director, The Economist Bookshop

Our hero, John Buckram, buys books. He lives in a London commuter area, where there is both a branch of a multiple chain of booksellers-cum-stationers and a smaller, privately owned enterprise which concentrates on books and has a wider (if idiosyncratically-selected) range of stock.

John Buckram patronises both establishments from time to time: he also makes use of similar shops during his City lunch breaks. He will patronise each of these establishements as mood and opportunity take him; sometimes going in search of a gift, sometimes seeking a paperback for his younger daughter, sometimes an Open University text for his wife's mother, a car manual for his teenage son, or simply a current paperback novel for light entertainment.

He probably exemplifies many a regular, if not totally addicted, book buyer: he visits the shops he knows, has a fairly precise idea of what he wants, occasionally asks advice of the booksellers he sees, and every now and then places a special order where his need is an exact one.

What we must observe about this paragon, for the purposes of considering the nature of direct mail bookselling, is how much he does for himself which he could not do were he being supplied by mail. He usually serves himself. He pays for what he buys through the simplest method of all: the cash register on the desk. He doesn't often place costly single copy orders: the chances are that if he can't find what he has in mind, then another title, or another conveniently close shop, will satisfy him. instead.

Suppose that our hero, in early middle life, his family growing up, decides to exercise his talents away from the yo-yo existence of the London commuter: away, with the benefit of an unexpected legacy, to a remote part of Scotland. There, sheep far outnumber people and life appears to be slower, more peaceful, more contemplative. Not a decision everyone would make; but our hero is not an ordinary member of society. He is a regular bookbuyer.

In seclusion, his need for books increases, if anything. He has the mobile library at his disposal, but lifelong habits of ownership, not temporary use, stay with him. His nearest bookshop is forty five miles away, along undulating single track roads, and its stock is small and unpredictable; far different from the choice offered him on his Saturday wanderings near London, or in his lunch time shopping in the City. How now is he to secure his car manual, his Open University text, his guide to winemaking, his light paperback reading?

John Buckram's dilemma

He is left with three choices: to fall back on the library, to do without, or to find a mail order bookseller. And that is where his bookseller's problems begin. By post, Buckram cannot serve himself. Payment must either be in advance, with his order, (rarely exactly the right amount) or his retailer must give him credit and bear the cost of both credit and collection. Errors can occur much more readily, for Buckram is not there to see the wrong title taken from the shelf, and when it arrives he suffers both the frustration of not having the wanted book and the annoyance of having to return the wrong one.

The best of booksellers cannot, as through Buckram's own eyes, select the alternative to the wanted title which is not in stock. Buckram, not rich or spendthrift, tends to be price-conscious; so that the unit cost of his selections is low, thus affording his supplier little cash margin out of which to meet the cost of mail order service. Unless his supplier is unwittingly subsidising Buckram's business out of his self-service, on-the-doorstep customers, Buckram is likely to find few booksellers willing to provide by post the facilities he once knew as a near-Londoner.

John Buckram's problems are a warning to those who feel that direct mail bookselling means providing by post the same facilities, at equal profit, as can be secured by making the same sales across a counter. It represents one extreme form of direct mail bookselling.

The many facets of direct mail bookselling

Since 'direct mail bookselling' means different things to different people, let us try to establish how many facets it has. First–'Buckram' bookselling. The supply by post to individuals of a variety of low cost articles, selected by them from the book trade's celebrated, vast storehouse of titles, frequently to special order at great internal cost, if not also at poor discounts; with complications of cash collection, cost of packing, posting and overall administration. Then–and not least– the cost of correspondence. Most people who buy books are literate–and Buckram is no exception. When he places an order, he finds it convenient to remind his supplier of all the titles already on order and still to be supplied (so far as he can remember). This way madness and order-duplication lie.

Second–at the other extreme–book club bookselling and similar types of massively-promoted direct mail selling. Here the entrepreneur offers a narrow choice of titles in alluring or lurid terms to a public which, once signed on, commits itself to a minimum number of selections (how effectively enforced?) and thus, by virtue of the economies of scale, which result from repeatedly selling to the same audience, can produce healthy profits for those able and willing to undertake the risk. 'Direct', here, means manufacturer to consumer, using no retailer.

Third—specialist publishing/bookselling and specialist bookselling. We describe 'publishing/bookselling' as the activities of those firms who have a domination of a particular field—architecture, numismatics, philately spring to mind—or a near-domination, as in the case of the principal legal publishers—and a clearly-definable and reachable market. Within such fields the distinction between publishing and bookselling is far narrower, (as also are many of the discounts paid to other booksellers). By specialist bookselling we mean the company which, though not itself in publishing, and carrying a range of stock from a wide variety of sources, confines itself to a particular subject area or group of subject areas.

Between these two lies a rogue element—the publisher who pays trade discounts of a kind, but at the same time deliberately pursues a direct sales policy in an attempt to have the best of both worlds. His support from booksellers is poor, so he sits in a state of righteous indignation about the shortcomings of his retailers while directly competing with them, usually making his own distributive systems less efficient in the process.

To consolidate what we have offered so far: at one extreme, Buckram bookselling—the attempt to offer all books by post to all people, an enterprise unlikely to succeed unless it is subsidised by other parts of the operation or helps meet its overheads during seasonal trading troughs. Then, colour supplement bookselling: clubs and other retailers offering heavily-promoted titles from a relatively narrow range to a public which, once gained, can be counted on to go on buying sporadically if not regularly. Then areas of specialist interest where publishers and/or booksellers can sell by mail to groups of buyers who can be reached with comparative ease and low cost.

Counting the cost

For most booksellers it will be in this last group that the opportunities lie, *if at all.* A note of caution must be sounded. Postal and clerical costs (the mail order bookseller finds himself needing clerical staff where previously he employed only sales assistants) have risen out of all proportion to book prices in recent years. Some compensation can be secured by using out-of-centre premises for mailing activity, but this may increase supply delays and increase problems of communication.

The bookseller who seriously contemplates mail order sale must have an awareness of a number of sales promotion techniques. He must have a means of maintaining a mailing list, and, at today's cost levels, a ruthless method of pruning dead wood from it. He must know what advertising will reach what market—for which purpose, Willing's *Press guide* is a must. He must familiarise himself with the list-brokers, IBIS and the rest, who claim to offer sets of names and addresses of individuals or institutions with particular interests. He must have internal systems able to record incoming orders, to refer to them when necessary between placement and completion, and systems for recording orders for non-stock items.

In that context, he must try to reach an agreeable compromise between carrying too much stock and minimising his special orders, which are slow to arrive, internally costly and seldom profitable except at high unit costs.

He will need an effective love-hate relationship with the GPO. He will need an understanding of world-wide postal regulations (the *Post Office guide* is the Bible), of franking meters, of packing boards and of packers.

He will need to know well the bookseller-orientated publishers in his selected field, or those whose fields include his selection, so that, should he see an opportunity to offer a particular title to a particular group, he will with ease be able to secure supplies of leaflets overprinted with his name, or contributions in the way of advertising to any catalogues he produces.

Catalogues

The compilation of catalogues, whether specialist or seasonal, is a subject in itself and is dealt with later in this chapter. What can be said here is that rising costs make the most modest catalogues a dubious proposition for the mail order bookseller of today.

The mail order bookseller can sell far more cheaply by concentrating on leaflets for individual books (supplied without charge by most publishers)—the leaflets, not the books—but then of course the maximum sales potential is far lower, too. But on balance, at current costs, this is likely to be less unattractive than the compilation of and despatch of ambitious catalogues—which may bring prestige but not profit. You can't pay bills with prestige.

Basic advice: a summary

In a summary as short as this it is best to conclude by offering advice of a very basic kind. First: if you intend to enter a new area of trading, be sure that it will not present you with problems which you cannot solve; or that if it will, you can afford to pay to have them solved, and that your existing business will not suffer in the process.

If you are to incur promotional costs, will they justify the net profitability of the extra business you will secure? Will the demands made on you personally by the new business be demands you can meet?

Lastly, remember that the mail order bookseller lacks one of the most potent of all sales promotion techniques: he cannot offer goods at bargain prices. In the book trade we compete on service, not price. (Resale price maintenance has been declared not to be against the public interest.) When we seek to promote sales, we are deprived of one of the most potent techniques of doing so. And so we should be: the techniques of the bazaar are not those of one of the commodities most precious to a continuing civilisation.

CATALOGUES

by Leonard S Fearnley, Founder and Director, Book Promotion Services Ltd

Publishers' catalogues

It must be obvious that catalogues are a vital part of the book scene. For how else could publishers bring their wide range of products to the notice of far-flung academics, librarians and booksellers? Certainly not by press advertising and the sprinkling of reviews alone.

Publishers spend a vast sum on the production of catalogues; their size, shape and presentation being as individualistic and varied as the wares they contain. Most are designed to inform; some to sell. Few are aimed at the final consumer, in that they generally cover a wide variety of subjects without meeting–and concentrating upon–the specific needs and interests of the individual.

Booksellers know all about publishers' catalogues for, with the *Bookseller,* they provide the storehouse of information on which their stock-in-hand is primarily based. Booksellers are always annoyed when they fail to receive a publisher's latest catalogue; sometimes they have difficulty in tracing the one desperately needed; and usually they become very angry when they get an unsolicited bulk supply.

Booksellers have frequently expressed the desire that publishers' catalogues should be produced to a standard cover size, with spine-titling for quick reference. This principle would certainly facilitate the possibility of publishers' catalogues being bound-up together, by subject, for selective distribution.

Some publishers' catalogues–covering specialised subjects– are distributed by them to clearly defined mailing-lists of known or potential buyers. Frequently, though not always, these invite a direct response to the publisher, who is thus able to assess the profitability of a distribution and the relative popularity of the included titles, and so to decide which of the various lists he has mailed are worth repeating.

Generally speaking, the average consumer is more interested in a broad picture of availability within a particular field of interest than in individual publishers' catalogues. In the absence of such lists he must write to all the relevant publishing houses for assistance; and this can be a very time-consuming and frustrating process.

Booksellers' catalogues

The bookseller, by producing his own collective lists, can provide an extremely useful service for his customers, which will also attract new ones; for catalogues, themselves, can be advertised to the public. Catalogues are a very effective medium for taking the bookshop to the people, but only if they present the appropriate image, are not too literary in approach, and set out to sell rather than just to inform.

A sad thing about most book catalogues is that, in an age when colour in advertising has come to stay, they seldom reproduce in colour the splendid book jackets into which so much creativity and expense has been poured. Imagine a bookshop's displays without them. Even public libraries find them worth preserving and they are not in the business of selling, yet.

Knowing that a large proportion of the adult population never enters a bookshop is it not shameful that these colourful and often beautiful 'silent salesmen' are kept indoors? The huge success of the book clubs emphasises the point.

Do's and don'ts

The problem, of course, is expense. Some ten years ago a leading bookseller costed for us, at £500, the overheads alone of putting together his

Christmas catalogue. To this had to be added production and distribution costs. And that was a decade ago!

But catalogues need not be expensively produced to be effective, so long as they are imaginative. A carefully compiled and legibly laid out listing, with pithy descriptions and, preferably, illustrations (using publishers' half-tone blocks or line drawings), sent to the right people, at the right time, is often more profitable than a full-colour job distributed indiscriminately. It is even forgiveable to adopt the 'first person' approach–'I am pleased to recommend, etc'. You must experiment and check the response, so that you know where you have succeeded in achieving your objective, of profit, or goodwill, or both.

Always consider including at least one very high-priced book; just a few sales could cover your costs at a stroke. And don't fail to enclose perhaps just one publisher's superbly produced prospectus, to give colour to your mailing.

There is a very good economic case for promoting a limited number of titles rather than a wide range–for you must be prepared to back-up your promotion by carrying available stocks to meet the expected demand. But 'catalogues'–and this was the subject of my brief– suggests a substantial selection, whether general or confined to one subject.

The economics

Confronted with the task of increasing the mail-order turnover (and profit) of a well-known bookshop, the writer soon discovered that the only way to make professionally-produced catalogues a viable proposition was to print long runs, with publishers contributing in support of their books. It was also necessary to explore the most potentially rewarding additional outlets for their distribution, as well as mailing regular customers.

It followed naturally that book catalogues could better be financed, compiled, produced and promoted from a central point, in the interests of all booksellers. One set of overheads, and large print runs–at reduced unit costs– would justify high quality production techniques. This would be a daunting task for any independent bookseller, even the largest, for today's costs can demand too high a return to justify the expense.

BPS book guides

Book Promotion Services was founded in 1964, with the initial objective of producing collective book guides (we never call them catalogues) in large quantities and usually in full colour, for use by booksellers—large, medium and small—anywhere in the world where British books were sold. Approximately five million have been distributed since commencement—through bookshops, public libraries, educational establishments, and other natural outlets suggested by the subject under consideration.

Publishers contribute towards production costs on a 'per entry' basis, scaled according to the total distribution achieved. Booksellers buy in bulk, at prices well below production cost; and any balance is supplied in bulk (free of charge) to libraries and other organisations which have applied.

Our book guides usually carry a nominal cover price, so that booksellers can, if they wish, sell them over the counter; thus recovering a proportion of their outlay immediately. Booksellers are sent advance details (arranged by publisher) of the books to be included; publishers are sent the names of participating booksellers and other outlets.

Fifty different book guides have been produced to date and the following titles give some indication of the range: *Ships, sailing and the sea; Horses and riding; Popular paperbacks; Travel; London; Computers;* and *Parenthood.* Some details of how we handle and distribute three of our guides, now established as 'hardy perennials', are given below:

What shall I read? —a guide to new books for young people of all ages and interests. Produced in full colour and distributed during October, this guide is mailed direct to 42,000 school and college librarians and teachers, at home and abroad, as well as being supplied in bulk to booksellers and public libraries. Those sent to schools incorporate a catalogue service for teachers and librarians, whereby they may apply to BPS for publishers' catalogues which particularly interest them. Some 26,000 publishers' catalogues have been requested since the service was introduced, four editions ago. Teachers are also offered free bulk supplies of *What shall I read?* for distribution to parents and pupils, usually at special 'book' events.

The schools' edition contains the names and addresses of 'ready, willing and able suppliers', ie booksellers who, by ordering a minimum 500 copies for their own use, and by agreeing to service resulting orders, qualify for inclusion. The 'trade' edition has an order form in place of the publishers' catalogue service, and does not contain the full list of suppliers. Fifty booksellers participated in the 1974 (ninth annual) edition, each receiving a supply bearing his own name and address on the front cover. Total distribution—1974 edition—100,000.

Books for business executives and business students (BBX) is produced in two colours (books in this category do not usually boast full-colour jackets) and distributed April/May. With the financial support of publishers it is sent to all members of the British Institute of Management, the Institute of Marketing, and similar bodies; to libraries–public, university, management and business studies. The direct distribution (approximately 110,000) includes the names and addresses of 'ready, willing and able suppliers', as with *What shall I read?* The total distribution–1975 (8th annual) edition–125,000.

Recommended new books This is the collective Christmas book guide, produced in full colour and available in October. Because many more titles are submitted by publishers than can be accommodated, their provisional lists are examined by a panel of booksellers, whose opinions are respected during the final process of selection. Quantities from 150,000 to 250 copies have been supplied to individual booksellers. Total distribution–1974 (eleventh annual) edition–325,000.

The first of a planned series of Topic Folders–*Books for your home*–was introduced in Spring 1975. It consisted of a six-page (A4 format) folder, printed in two colours (for economy) and containing approximately ninety books (new and established) for general family interest and appeal. With the co-operation of Book Tokens Ltd, who advertised in the folder, it was distributed door-to-door by many booksellers with Book Tokens reimbursing 50 per cent of the costs. Total distribution–200,000.

Due to the need expressed by booksellers to concentrate their promotional efforts on fewer books, the format of *Books for your home* was adopted for the 1975 Christmas book guide. This was produced in full colour, with descriptions and large reproductions of a maximum 100 jackets and the front-page headline–'Here are 100 new books which people will be talking about, buying, reading–and giving–this Christmas'.

The target distribution was 500,000–through 150/200 outlets–with Book Tokens Ltd again assisting with door-to-door distribution costs. *Books for Christmas* cost booksellers less than a quarter the price of the stamp needed to post it!

Continuing need

For as long as the output of British publishers continues at anything like the rate of 30,000 new titles each year, there will be an urgent need for booksellers—in their own interest—to produce selective catalogues for the enlightenment of their customers, existing and potential.

I hope that, similarly, there will be a growing awareness of the need for collective, more general book guides, taking the bookshop to the people as the first step towards persuading them—in *their* interests—to make more regular contacts with you, by personal visit, or by post.

KEYNOTES

- **Local press advertising should be tied to something specific like 'Back to School' or a major new title.**
- **Book Tokens Ltd will pay half the cost of an advert for tokens. This sort of advert also reminds local people of your existence for half the usual price.**
- **Without directly offering a quid pro quo, reward the local newspaper that treats books at length editorially with some advertising from time to time.**
- **Keep copy and layout simple.**
- **Try to adjoin editorial matter.**
- **Don't be afraid of white space.**
- **Advertising copy must clearly show why someone should buy the book being featured.**
- **The newspaper will always set your copy for you.**
- **Don't be afraid to include an advert whose layout you particularly like with your order and add: do it like that please.**
- **Direct mail can mean either the attempt to offer all books by post to all people; or book club selling by-passing the retailer; or specialist subject bookselling. For most booksellers only the last is likely to be viable.**
- **Mailing lists must be kept ruthlessly accurate and up-to-date.**

- Willings Press Guide and the Post Office Guide are essential tools for the mail-order bookseller.
- Selling by catalogues is a very expensive operation. Publishers leaflets are a much cheaper way of doing it.
- Think twice before plunging into mail order. Having costed everything realistically, can you still make a profit? Have you the resources and space, staff, etc to do it?
- Catalogues need colour in this day and age.
- Try to include one or two highly priced books when compiling a catalogue.
- Don't try to include too many titles: you will need back-up stock for everything advertised.
- Long print runs alone can bring down the cost of producing catalogues.
- Book Promotion Services produce co-operative catalogues, with publishers paying title entry charges and the bookseller buying in bulk at below production cost as a result.

9 BOOK TOKENS: A VITAL PROMOTIONAL AID

By John Brushfield,
Marketing Manager, Book Tokens Ltd

The British Book Token Scheme came into being in 1932, after six years germination following the original idea. It was the brainchild of a publisher, the late Harold Raymond, who was distressed by the fact that none of his friends was willing to give books as Christmas presents, due to the difficulty of choosing for other people.

Birth of a sickly child

Very few booksellers were interested in the idea and none could see how the scheme could possibly pay its way. When it was eventually launched, a founder member was W H Smith & Son, who gave the scheme the boost it needed; for with their large number of branches, Book Tokens became exchangeable throughout a large part of the country.

Growing up

In its early days, the scheme was run by the National Book Council. In 1943, a company with limited liability was formed: Book Tokens Ltd, owned by the Booksellers Association. As the business developed, it became necessary for it to have separate management and the first full-time manager was appointed in 1945.

The whole trade benefits

Although owned by the Booksellers Association, the success of the company has been, and continues to be, of benefit to both the publishing and retailing sides of the trade in producing more book sales, since its board of directors has included booksellers and publishers. The board is unpaid and meets at regular intervals. The whole object of Book Tokens is to sell more books.

Highly successful business

From its small beginnings, Book Tokens Ltd had developed into a substantial and successful commercial operation, with sales to the public of over £3,000,000 pa by 1976. A highly professional, full-time team of about fifteen people is involved in running the company.

Booksellers clearing house

One spin-off from the comapny's success has been the establishment and running by Book Tokens Ltd of a Clearing House for booksellers. This is a quite separate operation and involves handling, tabulating and making payment of booksellers' accounts with publishers, *at no cost* to the bookseller or publisher.

By accounting centrally in this way, a bookseller need write only one cheque to cover payments to, maybe, hundreds of publishers, leaving the Clearing House to re-distribute each month the appropriate amounts. In 1975 the annual turnover of the Clearing House was in the region of £24,000,000.

THE SCHEME AND ITS BENEFITS TO BOOKSHOPS

To this day there is some confusion in the trade about how the Book Token Scheme works, many booksellers still believing that Book Tokens Ltd benefits from a discount on the value of sales, when in fact it does not.

It simply acts as an organiser and transmitter of money between booksellers for their sales and exchanges. The chart demonstrates what happens to the money from a £1 token sale. It shows how the original bookseller selling the token retains 12-1/2 per cent of the value as a commission on the sale. This 12-1/2 per cent is paid for by the bookseller exchanging the token, who gives up 12-1/2 per cent from whatever discount he is getting from the publisher of the exchanged book. If this is 33 per cent, he is making a net gain of 20-1/2 per cent.

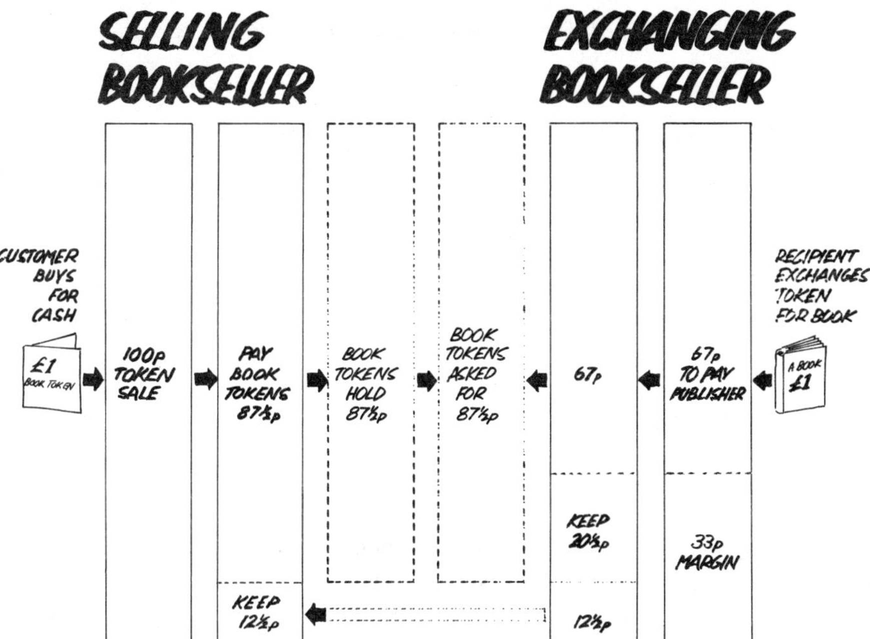

Note: The terms for the book exchanged for the token (above) are, of course, only for illustration purposes. The margin may well vary, depending on the publisher concerned and the type of book.

Benefits from exchanging

Although there is a reduced discount to the exchanging bookseller, there are a number of reasons that make book token business valuable:

Virtually all exchanges give a bookshop book sales that they would not otherwise have made. Obvious gift alternatives such as competitive token schemes compete strongly. Cash or cheque alternatives might be spent anywhere. A gift of a book token keeps the money in the book trade.

Stock is moved quicker–particularly post-Christmas. In this slack period about £1,000,000's worth of Christmas book tokens are exchanged. Research in 1970 showed that about 70 per cent of these were exchanged for hardback, non-fiction books. It is certain that some normally slow moving books are included in these exchanges.

Cash is frequently added to the value of a token. Research in 1970 showed that 65 per cent of the sample had paid more than the token value for the book they wanted.

Most book tokens are given to the young. Encouraging children and teenagers into bookshops must be of long term help to the trade. A satisfied customer will come back again and again and the principle of 'catch 'em young' still holds good.

Benefits from selling

For the bookshops that sell more book tokens than they exchange, the superficial limitation of only a 12-1/2 per cent discount obscures several important facts:

There is no capital tied up in stocking book token stamps. A nominal sum is involved in purchasing the cards, of course, but with current high interest rates, the cost of stocking book tokens is negligible compared with books or other products.

Book token sales provide a useful source of cash flow. Settlement is quarterly and thus any cash from sales can be used by the shop concerned for up to 3 months.

The profit generated from a small selling space is relatively high. A bookshop selling £1,000 worth of tokens per annum and devoting 2 square feet of counter space to display makes 12-1/2 per cent or £125= £62.75 gross profit per square foot. Repeated Charter Group economic surveys show the average bookshop profit per square foot of floor space to be £9–£12.

The ideal situation

By and large, the ideal situation is for a shop to sell and exchange roughly the same amount of business. This results in their getting what are in effect normal terms on those books they exchange through the book token scheme, since they are effectively passing on to *themselves* the 12-1/2 per cent allowed on token sales. A further look at the chart on page 95 should make this clear.

HOW THE COMPANY'S COSTS ARE MET

Although Book Tokens Ltd gets nothing from the stamp value, it does obtain income–its only regular income–from the sale of the cards on which the stamps are stuck. These are sold to booksellers, who in turn sell them to members of the public at the same prices (in 1975) of four pence for standard cards and six pence for large cards, including the envelope and VAT.

Token cards income

The net value of selling the current requirement of over 2,000,000 cards per annum, after deduction of production and printing costs, storage, envelopes etc, is worth in the region of £40,000–£50,000 per annum. This goes towards the cost of company administration, overheads and especially promotion.

Money makes money

There are two more important sources of revenue that were never foreseen when the scheme was started. The first involves the liquidity, or cash in hand, between the purchase and redemption of book tokens. With current high interest rates, money is always earning its keep while it is held.

The second involves a small proportion of tokens that are bought but never exchanged; being mislaid, destroyed or forgotten. Over the years, between 1 per cent and 2 per cent of tokens have been shown to disappear in this way. Although there is always the possibility that they may reappear, the use of the capital involved has been to the benefit of the trade as a whole.

Some booksellers have expressed the view that cards should be supplied free, as Boots and W H Smith do for their voucher schemes. If this was done with book tokens, there would be virtually no money available for promotion (advertising, point-of-sale material, etc) and, in addition, money would need to be found to pay for the cost of producing over 2,000,000 cards per year; about £20,000–£30,000. In practice, research has shown that the few pence involved in buying cards are not large enough to inhibit more than a tiny proportion of purchasers; probably because the amounts are so small when current costs of greeting cards are taken into account.

BOOK TOKENS PROMOTE MORE BOOK SALES

By itself, a book token is only half way to being a product. It is in its capacity to be transformed into any book (rather like the chrysalis becoming the butterfly) that promotion can best be developed creatively. By book trade standards, a substantial amount of money is spent in promotion to the public; and because general book promotion (with only a few notable exceptions) is so fragmented, literary and in-bred in character, book tokens are a valuable help in quite simply extending the market of people to come to bookshops by bringing them to the attention of the public.

Type of promotional support

Promotional aids can be split into four main types:

1 National advertising
2 Local advertising support
3 In-store display material
4 Special offer promotions

1 National advertising

In recent years, national press advertising has been concentrated pre-Christmas, when about 30–40 per cent of sales occur. However, a recent development has been to continue the pre-Christmas advertising during the following spring and summer, with a view to improving year-round sales. Publications used include popular ones such as *Womans own, TV times, Reader's digest, Family circle*, plus other media, and reflect the fact that the majority of book tokens are bought by women, 90 per cent of whom are being reached by the advertising.

It is fair to say that it is very rare for any single book or group of books to receive this weight of promotion. Bearing in mind the heavy weight of advertising for book clubs and direct-selling companies, the book token advertising is particularly valuable to the retail trade, because it helps to remind the public of their local bookshops.

2 Local advertising support

In support of the national advertising outlined, several smaller spaces are offered to booksellers for use in their local papers, with part of the cost being met by Book Tokens Ltd. This ensures a repetition of the national advertising theme, while helping to support booksellers locally, where consumer purchases take place.

In the past, in the pre-Christmas period, 200–300 advertisements of this type have been used by booksellers. The subsidised scheme certainly helps them stretch their limited promotional budgets, while helping book tokens get maximum results from the co-ordination of national and local advertising.

One other means of local promotion concerns door-to-door distribution of special leaflets produced for this purpose. Booksellers are encouraged to arrange distribution of a book token leaflet (possibly including their own shop leaflet or letter) by using door-to-door distributors, or as an insert in local papers.

A substantial part of the cost of distribution is met by Book Tokens Ltd. Contact with distribution companies can be arranged and door-to-door costs are about £7–£9 per 1,000 households, making this an economic method of getting a bookshop better known locally, or for special seasonal promotions. It is another example where practical help and financial support works both in Book Tokens' and local booksellers' interests.

3 In-store display material

One of the greatest 'wastes' of advertising occurs when people who have seen the advertising cannot find a shop selling the product, or, if they have found a shop, cannot see it displayed. A wide range of material is produced to help bookshops promote book tokens and this falls into two main groups: material that displays token card designs, and posters, showcards or streamers that reflect the current advertising theme.

In the former group, the two main alternatives are wire dispensers or plastic pocketed wallets. In the latter, a variety of material is available, including mobiles, door stickers, book crowners, bookmarks, etc. To date, most material has been supplied free, although there is a small carriage charge for the wire dispensers. As pointed out earlier it is the revenue from card sales that makes this possible.

Card designs

It would be very easy to overlook the importance of featuring a good range of attractive token card designs as a display aid. After all the card is *almost* the product, and because a book token is always bought as a gift for others, the packaging of the gift in an attractive, colourful way should never be forgotten. Booksellers usually have between 20–30 designs from which

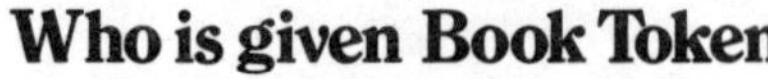

Who is given Book Tokens

Research has consistently shown that about two-thirds of tokens are given to teenagers and under.
More males are given book tokens than females.

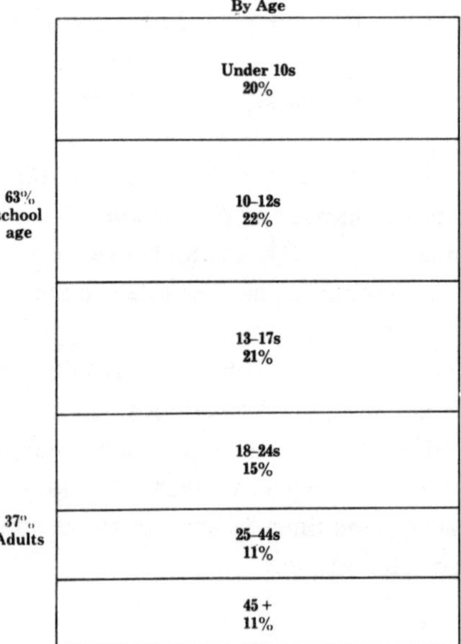

to choose, with various designs of appeal to children, adults, academics etc. It is difficult to satisfy all tastes, and every bestseller is at the same time another bookshop's worst seller. It is worth pointing out that designs are chosen with consumer appeal in mind, *not* bookseller appeal, and many cards are subjected to research among housewives before being chosen.

The standard range of cards includes traditional subjects and also some attractive fold-out friezes that are in themselves a small present. The latter, together with the larger designs, were introduced especially for children; with stories, puzzles and information in each. This enhances the gift at the time of opening—often when shops are shut (see illustration).

The token area in which the stamps are stuck was designed by banknote printers, Bradbury & Wilkinson, in order to enhance the value of what may be quite an expensive purchase. It should not be forgotten that in any gift purchase, the giver must feel satisfied as well as the recipient!

Some booksellers are inclined to order a small selection of cards to offer their customers, which in turn can lead to consumers' criticising the poor choice of designs. The attitude to the choice of cards ought to be no different to that adopted to the selection of books offered by a good bookseller.

4 Special offer promotions

From time to time, promotions are devised which are designed to attract the attention of the public (and particularly non book-buyers) to book tokens. In addition to some simple and straightforward competitions, with various value book token prizes, a new promotion was introduced in the spring of 1976 offering 6 historical bookplates free to anyone buying a book token.

Kits were made up and dispatched to all accounts. they included a showcard-cum-dispenser, poster, leaflets and a quantity of bookplates. The quantity was based on each shop's 1975 sales and should have been sufficient supply for one month plus a 50% increase. A reserve stock was held for reorders, or where the original supply was inaccurate. The promotion was advertised in colour in 5 major consumer magazines.

RESEARCH INFORMATION ABOUT BOOK TOKENS

A substantial amount of research information has been obtained about book token buyers in recent years. As mentioned earlier, as a gift line, purchase is more often than not by women, particularly housewives. This is understandable because nearly two-thirds of all book tokens are given to the under-seventeens.

Who is given Book Tokens?

Age	%
Under 10s	20
10–12	22
13–17	21
18–20	8
21–24	7
25–44	11
45–64	8
65+	3

It is natural to see why tokens should be a popular choice during school years, with changing interests difficult to monitor.

Who buys book tokens?

Boys are given more book tokens than girls, perhaps confirming the traditional view that it is more difficult to know what to give boys.

Although buyers come from all age groups and social classes, book tokens are more likely to be bought by people between 35–44, the better off, and the better educated. However, as with most products sold, the majority of purchases are still made by the C1, C2 lower-middle and skilled classes who comprise the majority of the population.

The uncle/aunt, nephew/niece, relationships are the most likely for givers and recipients. More people are likely to have purchased a book token in the south of Britain than the north, particularly in the south-east. It is possible that this is simply a reflection of the fact that there are more bookshops per head of population in the south. Most book tokens are exchanged for hardback, non-fiction.

When do sales occur?

Sales and exchanges data is compiled by bookshops and sent to Book Tokens Ltd, on a quarterly basis. A fairly consistent pattern of selling between the four quarters has emerged over the past few years and the most recent figures show the following:

Period	*% of sales*
Feb-Apr	14
May-July	17
Aug-Oct	21
Nov-Jan	48
	100

From more detailed information obtained from some booksellers it would seem that the Christmas share of the relevant quarter is probably between 30-40 per cent, leaving 60-70 per cent fairly evenly spread throughout the rest of the year for other forms of gift purchase, notably birthdays. Other minor peaks occur for school prizes and Easter.

Range of account size

Booksellers have to be members of the Booksellers Association before they can sell book tokens, but equality in membership obscures a wide variation in sales success. The following table illustrates an analysis of sales based on 1973/4 data and shows the relationship between the percentage of accounts and percentage of sales turnover of 2,000 independent bookshops.

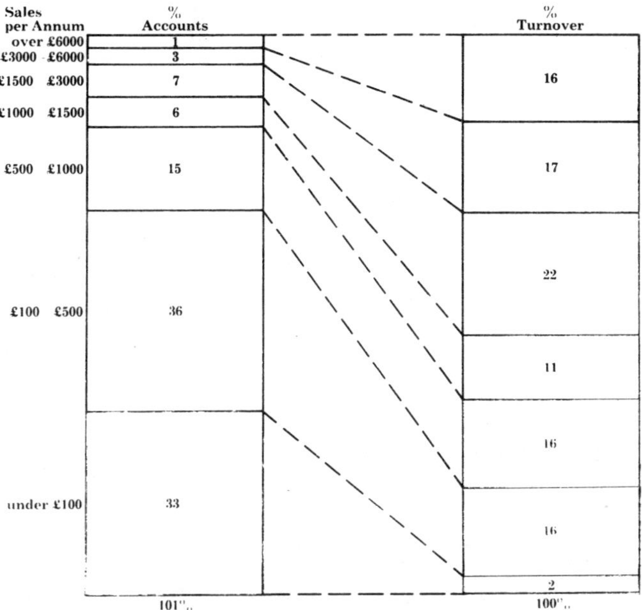

From this table, it can be seen that 69 per cent of the independent bookshops produce only 18-1/2 per cent of the sales turnover. These will be among those paying the minimum subscription to the Booksellers Association.

At the other end of the scale, the top 11 per cent of accounts are producing 55-1/2 per cent of the sales turnover and include the well known names of the trade's major bookshops.

However, the capacity to develop greater sales, with good in-store display and supporting advertising, exists just as much for the smallest accounts as for the largest. There are many examples of previously uninterested bookshops who have doubled or trebled their sales by quite modest use of displays, *showing* their customers that they sold book tokens.

HOW TO GET THE BEST OUT OF BOOK TOKENS

There is a tendency for booksellers to imagine that every member of the public knows about book tokens and is aware that they sell them. This is just not true. Bearing in mind that many book tokens are bought by people who are, at best, irregular book buyers, successful promotion may well improve book sales to the same customers. We can be certain at least that 2,000,000 purchasers means 2,000,000 recipients–a total of 4,000,000 customers brought into bookshops each year via book tokens alone.

In addition, commonsense tells us that the sale of a book token will rarely if ever be at the expense of a book, but it does stop the trade losing the business. So the major points to get the best out of this situation are:

1 Have a display of cards visible near the cash desk so that it can be seen by customers.

2 Have a sticker on the door to tell *passers-by* that 'book tokens are sold and exchanged here'.

These are two rather passive points because they both assume that the customer will come to the bookshop anyway. We recognise, and so should bookshops, that good marketing involves going looking for business. Obvious ways that are used by many of our customers each year include:

3 Take advantage of the subsidised book token advertisements in the local press.

4 Use the book token leaflets in subsidised door-to-door distribution and make sure a promotional leaflet for the bookshop is included with it, and a sketch showing the shop's location. This can be seasonally orientated, or devoted to a few or many books (eg Leonard Fearnley's book catalogues).

5 Occasionally, devote part of the window display to book tokens, using the attractive (and expensive) free display material. By all means combine it with books–the two are synonymous.

6 Tackle local schools, clubs, Sunday schools, and organizations about the use of book tokens as prizes, incentives, leaving presents etc. Material and help is available from Book Tokens Ltd for this purpose.

7 Devise and publicise small incentives in the form of simple competitions or events with book tokens as prizes. A modest sum will often be given to bookshops by Book Tokens Ltd in exchange for the publicity.

8 Use the free book token bookmarks as handouts from the shop, bag stuffers etc.

Australia

The Australian Book Token scheme differs only slightly from the UK one. It was established as recently as 1973. It is operated by Book Tokens Pty Ltd, a subsidiary of the Australian Booksellers Association.

Booksellers purchase book tokens in the form of printed vouchers at face value less 10%. They make a profit of 10% on the sale of tokens.

The redeeming bookseller when presenting tokens to Book Tokens Pty Ltd gets paid 87-1/2% of the face value–thereby having relinquished 12-1/2% of his profit margin on books supplied in exchange for book tokens.

The 2-1/2% difference between the discount allowed to the purchasing bookseller and the amount paid to the redeeming bookseller is retained by Book Tokens Pty Ltd to cover operating costs.

In view of the late establishment of the scheme, many booksellers had operated their own book token schemes. However the ABA operation has rapidly gained acceptance, is now firmly established and is considered a success.

KEYNOTES

- **Book Tokens is the hub through which the seller and exchanger of the token adjust their transaction. The seller gets 12-1/2% of the value of the token sold, the exchanger the discount allowed him by the publisher on the particular book <u>less</u> 12-1/2%.**
- **Tokens create sales.**
- **Book Tokens Ltd will share the cost of local paper advertising with the bookseller.**
- **Book Tokens Ltd will share the cost of distribution of door-to-door leaflets which remind the recipients of the shop's existence apart from advertising tokens.**
- **Nearly 2/3 of all tokens are given to the under 17's.**
- **Book Tokens, and Book Tokens Ltd's sales material, must be displayed to achieve optimum sales.**
- **Persuade schools and other bodies to give book tokens as prizes.**

10 KNOW YOUR COMMUNITY

By Martyn Goff
The Ibis Bookshop, Banstead

Anyone deciding to open a new bookshop needs to make a very careful study of the proposed district. Has it a good mix of social classes? Schools? Colleges? A reasonable cross-section of age groups?

To do this requires a combination of desk research and field work. The former would mainly be done at the local council offices; the latter in local pubs, cafés and shops. Stand in a High Street for an hour or two: you will soon discover which parts of it are most used, which is the 'golden shopping' section, where a bus stop or bank persuades people to cross the road. The council office may give you some idea of how much a particular street serves as a catchment area for the surrounding towns or villages; the publican will quickly add to your knowledge. All this is essential for the person about to open; it's equally essential for the bookseller who is already there if he hasn't carried out this sort of survey already.

The new or existing bookseller, having acquired the basic information, should then move on to the Bank Manager and the Editor of the local newspaper. The former will not necessarily yield key information until trust has been established between manager and client; the latter may be too busy or just not approachable, in which case one of his reporters will serve as well. Apart from giving information, these two can assist the shop: the first by putting business its way; the second by publicising it.

A sharp, detailed assessment of who is living in a radius of five miles of the shop, where they do their shopping and what sort of money they have for disposal after the necessities of life have been provided is the first step. Contact with the organisations that service those people is the second. Head Teachers should be visited regardless of whether it is hoped to supply the particular school with books. A link with the school can be established by offering prizes for creative literary work or assistance in producing the school magazine. Visits of classes to the bookshop to see a particular range of books or a small exhibition can be arranged. Book tokens as prizes can be advised; and special times for the children to come to the shop (when it is otherwise quiet) to choose their books. Or the prize-winners can just come to the shop to choose their prizes which are afterwards invoiced to the school, a list of names and amounts having been sent in advance.

On such a visit the bookseller may also suggest to the Head Teacher that he sets up a bookselling stall at the next Parent-Teacher meeting. 'Give a book to the School Library' is almost unfailing on these occasions: no parent wants to let down his child by being the one who didn't donate a book! Although the term 'Head Teacher' has been used, such a visit can be made instead to the Head of the English Department who is often more concerned with books and their use than the Head. But any or all of these things —and some others not listed here—may arise once the contact has been established; and similar contacts with every school in the vicinity set up a network along which much business may flow, and the means by which the growing generations are urged to visit their local bookshop.

Such contacts are equally important with other local groups, bodies and associations. The bookseller can hardly join the Women's Institute (if a man), the Rotary (if a woman) and the several hundred other organisations that exist in most districts. But he or she can give a talk to the Women's Institutes—not, of course, directly on his shop but on some subject connected with books: meetings with famous authors; stories about bestsellers; literary gossip of a general nature; or speak at a Rotary lunch. He can join the local tennis club or archaeological society or church (he can't of course be a member of all the different churches that may exist locally, but he can know all the vicars and priest, can send them an occasional book to be reviewed in their parish magazines). He can join the horticultural society or the art group, present an occasional prize to their annual shows; and be credited for having done so. He can, and must, become part of the local community.

Above all the bookseller must make early and strong contact with his local public librarian. Both are serving the same community; each can complement the work of the other in many ways: exhibitions, lists, encouragements of local literary societies, etc. This is just as true where the bookseller has no library licence as it is when he is supplying the library with books.

The bookseller's assessment of the income and age groups of his local community will show him what to stock; his contacts with some of the groups and people listed above will help him publicise the shop and its stock. If there is a local golf club, then he should stock golf books *and* tell the Club Secretary or Professional about them: that showcard from the publisher is just the thing for the clubhouse notice board. A visit or persuasive letter should do the trick.

In every community there will be people who visit the local bookshop automatically, people who only call there at Christmas time or if a book is needed for school or evening classes, and the majority who are not consciously aware that it is there. One way of getting at the last group is to show other goods in the window that have been borrowed from local traders: sports gear to go with sports books, motoring accessories with car books and so on. Credit the other trader in a neat typewritten or letraset card next to the goods. Then suggest that the other trader in question might benefit his window designs by carrying associated books, and this time crediting the bookseller. In the first case people will look in the window who might not otherwise have done so; in the second people will become aware of the bookshop through reading its name and situation in other shop windows.

More expensive, and requiring much more organising, is house-to-house leaflet, list or catalogue distribution. This can either be of a co-operative catalogue, or a publishers' leaflet or hand-out with the bookseller's name overprinted or stamped, or something produced by the bookseller himself. All three can be delivered either by professional 'knock-and-drop' organisations, or members of the shop's staff earning some extra money, or boy scouts and the like. Production of one's own handbills and lists is expensive but not impossible. Carefully planned distribution of an offset litho leaflet for a coffee-table book or two to more wealthy streets can work, but it is a matter of trial and error and proceeding slowly.

Visits to local factories and offices can be productive in two different ways: first, many of them have small libraries of their own, featuring technical works connected with their trade or profession, and can be swayed to use the bookshop by promise (and fulfulment!) of good service. Secondly, they can very often be persuaded to give books rather than bottles of whisky as Christmas presents, the bookseller offering to pack and post on receipt of gift cards and names and addresses of recipients. This, it should be added, is a job for October or very early November, not December!

Other chapters in this book have emphasised the importance of good lighting, practical shop design, first class display. In all these, and not necessarily at great expense, the bookshop can and should get a reputation for being a leader. The most unusual display, the best-designed fascia board, strikingly lit windows accrete to the reputation of a shop over the years until the whole High Street look to it for leadership. Depending on situation, a very occasional poetry reading or talk by an author at least locally well-known, a modest evening party to celebrate some occasion of a literary nature, all these too will serve to single out the bookshop as different from, and more alive than the shops that always simply close at half past five. These are not gimmicks, and gimmicks should be used sparingly, but attempts to display the bookshop as a special service to the community without which it would be the poorer.

More ambitious booksellers can try literary lunches or dinners. These involve close contact with the publisher's publicity manager and rep, good relations with a local caterer, a flair for getting publicity in local newspapers and societies, and flawless organisation of tickets, payments and arrangements for the speaker's arrival, speech and departure. Whatever its pretensions, most districts will respond to the celebrity more quickly than the literary author, so be sure to press the publisher for that actor or actress, golfer or TV personality who is right in the public eye at the moment of the lunch. Even the Yorkshire Post, and Richard Douro who runs their splendidly attended lunches, never forgets this basic rule. Above all, and involving the bookshop totally, is the need for the smoothest possible arrangements for selling the author's books at the end of the lunch: it's no good having him or her near one door while everyone files out of another! If the bookseller is lucky he'll find a local customer or two who may well be willing to organise the meal and publicity for him (in collaboration with the publisher), but the book-*selling* bit must be his.

The bookshop, in short, must win a special place for itself in the community. This is easier if the bookseller is a local figure of some note: a councillor or chairman of the drama group, a regular contributor to the local paper or prominent Rotarian. While not lacking one whit of business acumen, he must feel and proclaim ideals that win for him a small but real place in the locality's heart: that way lies satisfaction and profit.

KEYNOTES

- **Study the district in depth.**
- **Contact your bank manager and the editor of the local newspaper: they really know the area.**
- **Establish contact with as many local organisations as possible.**
- **Contact all local schools whether you supply them with books or not.**
- **Put up a bookstall at PTA meetings.**
- **Join at least some local societies.**
- **Establish strong links with the local public library.**
- **Borrow window display accessories from other traders. Lend them books.**
- **Distribute house-to-house leaflets or catalogues.**
- **Get in touch with local industry. Bigger factories and units may have their own libraries. All businesses give some Christmas presents. Why not books next time?**
- **Get the reputation for being the leading local shop in new developments from lighting to marketing.**
- **If you have the resources, arrange literary lunches and dinners.**

11 THE ROLE OF THE BOOK CLUBS

By Dick Cripps
Creative Director, Book Club Associates

Man doth not live by bread only: The quotation is taken, of course, from the Great Bestseller (Deuteronomy 8.3). Unfortunately for the publishing and bookselling trades, there is no indication that the average man and woman supplement their diet of bread with a substantial intake of book reading.

As a nation we British–once we escape from the forced-feeding of book reading during our school years–do not turn *en masse* to books for our adult entertainment. Compared with the continentals, we have never been major consumers of books. And since the advent of television in the fifties, reading has had an even tougher uphill battle.

According to recent surveys we spend about half of our thirty eight hours of leisure time each week watching TV, and only a measly two hours a week reading books. And those are only *average* figures. About a third of the population never opens a book at all.

Bookshops–and the struggle for custom

But if the book reading habits of the British leave a lot to be desired, our book *buying* habits are even more depressing. Perhaps with one of the best free lending library services in the world to compete with, it isn't too surprising that bookshops have always had to struggle for customers.

When we talk about book buyers, we are referring to people who make a *habit* of buying books. Whether they are buying books for their own pleasure or as gifts for other people is not vitally important. What is important is that they call in at a book shop regularly. That they actually enjoy browsing through the shelves–and can be counted upon to make a purchase.

These people are—and always have been—in a minority. The Book Promotion Feasibility Study indicated that no less than '48 per cent of the adult population either never visit a bookshop, or visit a bookshop less frequently than once a month'.

The need for an evangelical approach

Clearly it is the problem of increasing the size of this minority which faces everyone who makes a living from selling books—publishers, booksellers and book clubs alike. There is a real need for an enthusiastic—evangelical if you like—approach to the problem. It is too easy to adopt a defeatist attitude about the situation and to complain that the book-buying market is of a fixed and limited size, and that too many people are trying to grab a piece of it for everyone to make a decent living.

Obviously there will always be a hardcore majority who will firmly resist buying any kind of book from anybody. But what about that huge potential 'fringe' market? The people who enjoy reading—whether it's an occasional paperback bought on holiday, or a book borrowed from the local library, or from a friend.

A gentle push, a little persuasive encouragement is often all that is needed to convert them into reasonably regular book buyers; people with the book buying *habit*. And it really doesn't matter who gives the push—publisher, bookseller or book club.

The weight of book club advertising

It is in this 'fringe' territory that book clubs have had their most telling effect. The sheer weight and scope of book club advertising (now around £3 million annually) has undoubtedly helped to increase the total size of the book-buying market.

Book clubs create new book-buyers

That really is the significant point. Book clubs have not selfishly helped themselves to a slice of the existing book-selling cake. By their efforts they have increased the size of the cake itself and that must mean that there are bigger slices available for everyone.

The outcome has been that people, who had hardly ever bought a book before, are becoming regular book buyers as a result of their membership of a book club. It really doesn't matter that their initial experience of book buying is with the book club they happened to have joined. From then on, the regular contact with information about books of all kinds which they enjoy as members, through monthly club bulletins, ensures that their interest in books will quite rapidly spread beyond the club to the wider range of reading which most good bookshops offer.

Apart from the book reviews in the 'heavyweight' daily and Sunday newspapers, which are read largely by that devoted minority of book lovers already referred to, the only major source of news about books and authors seen in our national media is that contained in book club advertising.

Publishers' publicity, of course, plays its part. But in the nature of things, with such a wide range of titles to promote (some 32,000 titles published each year), publishers' advertising money has to be spread very thinly. The big-name authors get the bulk of the attention—the rest hardly a mention.

Book club advertising

The volume and nature of book club advertising, on the other hand, ensures that many more books are read about, by many more people, in a far wider range of media—from Sunday supplements to supermarket magazines. Full colour pages, often two or three pages at a time, are taken in all the important and big circulation magazines and papers. Indeed, an eight-page book club advertisement feature, introduced by Frank Muir, was placed in the *Observer colour supplement.*

These advertisements are tightly packed with pictures of, and information about, currently available books on a wide range of topics and interests. Best-sellers are, of course, well in evidence. But so are many other titles in almost every kind of category—history, biography, travel, art, cookery, gardening, reference books, mystery and science fiction, and so on. Non-fiction is particularly well represented.

Often a book—particularly a non-fiction title—which has had limited publicity backing from its publishers, has been featured in a book club advertisement, with the result that there has been an increased demand throughout the trade.

Effect on book prices

It is not only in the area of book publicity that book clubs have come more and more in recent years to play a significant role. In a climate of constantly rising prices the existence of a bulk book club order for a particular new title has extended the print run and helped keep the unit price down to a level which would otherwise have hardly been possible. Alan Jenkins's best-selling book *The twenties*, for example, was competitively priced at £5 retail, mainly due to a substantial book club order. Without that order the retail price would certainly have been pushed up to around £6.50.

There have been many instances where an out-of-print title has been reprinted for the whole trade much sooner than would normally have been feasible due to a heavy book club order. John Prebble's *The high girders*; Stuart Piggott's *The druids* and *Easter Island* by Alfred Metraux are just a few of the titles which have benefited recently in this way.

Joint sponsorship

Joint sponsorship between publisher and book club is another hopeful trend which is making important new series and individual titles available to the whole retail trade at tellingly lower prices. The very popular *Kings and Queens of England* series, edited by Antonia Fraser, is a typical example of this kind of activity. More recently, the sumptuous *An illustrated history of England*, with pictures on every page and a foreword by Sir Arthur Bryant, is another.

More joint efforts of this kind are in the pipeline, and the appointment of a full-time commissioning editor, in one of the major book club groups, is an indication that this is a policy that is going to be pursued energetically, with obvious benefits to all.

National promotion benefits all

Clearly, there seems little likelihood in the near future of any major co-operative book publicity on the part of publishers. Perhaps too many individual interests—and certainly too many individual titles—make combined publicity too complicated to handle.

Booksellers for their part must, by definition, confine their publicity efforts in the main to local advertising and point-of-sale display.

It remains, then, with the book club movement to continue to carry the major weight of truly national promotion of books and the pleasure of reading. It is obviously in their own interest to do so.

But it is worth repeating that every new convert to regular book reading and even more important to regular book *buying* is a potential new market for everyone in the book trade.

KEYNOTES

- Book clubs have increased the size of the book market, particularly among the fringe public who don't often visit bookshops but can occasionally be tempted to buy a book.
- Book clubs' advertising reaches far larger numbers than anything publishers can afford to do.
- Book club orders help to lengthen the print run and so keep prices down.

12 CONTINENTAL WAYS AND METHODS

By D Richard Bowen

For a number of years now I have had the pleasure of representing some leading British publishers on the continent. On my travels I have had first-hand opportunity of observing some of the principal ways in which books (particularly bound books) are sold by retail booksellers in Western Europe, as well as studying some of the different methods used for sales promotion.

Books in English

Whilst English is not the native language of any country on the continental mainland of Europe, books in the English language enjoy an enviable reputation in many of them. Books in English are classified as 'Foreign books' in these countries, and in many bookshops the foreign books are placed in a department of their own. In some larger bookshops, however, all books—regardless of the language in which they are written—are classified by subject, much to the delight of specialists and collectors in particular.

Though several different languages are in active use on the mainland of Europe, it is of great significance that many of the language areas are in themselves very small; furthermore, the export of books published in some of these languages is very small indeed. Locally-published books tend to be fewer in number than might be expected, and books in English often fulfil a very real need. The fact that the English language has been widely taught in schools on the continent for the last quarter of a century has greatly helped the sale of books in English in this geographical area.

Paperbacks in the English language are often obtainable at kiosks, which are frequently found in many continental countries. These paperbacks are usually supplied by local distributing wholesalers who give a very comprehensive and nationwide service. Wholesalers similarly stock and distribute a limited number of bound books of a more popular nature, and furthermore are often prepared to obtain titles ordered by booksellers on behalf of their customers.

In most European countries there are many bookshops relative to the population. Of these bookshops only a small proportion sell significant numbers of books in English and an even-smaller proportion actually import directly from publishers in the United Kingdom. It is with this latter type of bookshop that we are concerned here.

As far as 'General' books are concerned, attractive coloured jackets (displayed face-outwards) greatly stimulate sales, and informative illustrations (preferably reproductions of colour-photographs) are of great importance to sales-at-sight. Books of this category are often sent out on approval by enterprising booksellers to public libraries, etc, with gratifying results. Academic books, which are more often sold purely on merit, are also sent out on approval by continental booksellers to selected customers—often on a regular basis.

Sales promotion methods

Over the past couple of decades continental booksellers have developed distinct and competitive sales promotion methods as far as 'Library-type' titles of general and academic interest are concerned, their promotion being aimed at academic specialists, collectors and sometimes enthusiasts, as well as the more traditional library, university, industrial and institutional customers. These sales promotional methods, which can be very costly yet very profitable for the booksellers, include the systematic mailing of:

Publishers' own catalogues and announcements.

Subject prospectuses, which are most often welcomed by bookseller and customer alike.

Punched-cards, one per book, often prepared by a group of booksellers, one per country.

Furthermore, telephone sales promotion is not unknown, especially as far as series or multi-volume works are concerned.

Whilst it is very difficult to obtain accurate and comprehensive statistics of the results obtained by each of these methods, it can initially be stated that the on approval system has worked very effectively in the past. This system has the advantage that the prospective customer can actually handle and inspect the book which he can then buy if he so wishes: as far as public libraries in particular are concerned, the book received on approval can be inspected with a view to a bulk purchase of that title for a group of libraries (eg in a large city, country or province). The disadvantage of this system lies in the fact that a customer can be inundated with on approval books—and sometimes with more than one copy of the same title, depending on the number of enterprising would-be suppliers that he may have!

Regarding the other sales promotion methods mentioned, the use of publishers' own catalogues and announcements has the advantage that the material is in the same language as the books described: the prices are normally converted rather easily into the local book prices prevailing by use of the booksellers' exchange-table for the currency concerned.

Subject prospectuses have the advantage of describing mostly books that are of interest only to the customer concerned, whereas individual-title prospectuses are very much to the point indeed.

Subject lists of new books (most often from more than one publisher) are usually compiled in the local language, and used to be more usual than they are nowadays. The decline in this form of sales promotion in some countries is doubtless due to the comparatively high cost of making shortish runs of such promotional material in a colourful, modern, attractive and selling style.

Punched cards

Punched cards, too, can be costly to make—not least from an editorial point of view, and the selection of books chosen has to be judicious as well as commercial. Books that are subjected to this promotional treatment should be of a certain minimum price, and this minimum price has increased quite rapidly since the inception of this method. The punched-card method has the advantage that no illustrations are expected nor even usually possible (thus limiting costs) as such cards are often made when a title is first announced—and the earlier the better, too!

Telephone sales promotion can work well in the case of serious and multi-volume works, but this method can be very time-consuming. Perhaps fully-computerised sales promotion (using one or more of the methods mentioned) of books will be commonly used before too long.

Competition in some specialised fields and in some of the less-densely populated countries of Western Europe can be very keen indeed, and many booksellers within this area have become superbly organised to supply the needs of their customers: books are obtained to order from almost anywhere in the world, and often many languages are spoken and used for correspondence within the precincts of one single bookshop.

Specialist booksellers

Quite naturally, too, there are many purely specialist booksellers on the continent, of whom some do not even have a shop as such, but operate almost entirely by mail order. Some of these specialists sell both new and antiquarian books in their particular subjects only, and are often mines of information. They frequently have 'standing order' type customers, and issue useful book lists which are of great bibliographical value.

Mark up

In spite of the fact that bookselling practice varies from country to country within Western Europe, it can generally be said that the continental bookseller is obliged to 'mark up' the foreign (and so English) books he sells so as to cover postage or freight costs, handling charges and other costs connected with importing; but libraries etc, are often granted some form of rebate. In many continental countries, books are subject to Value Added Tax too: whilst the actual amount of VAT varies, it can be as much as 17-1/2 per cent on the marked-up price.

It is unfortunate that it takes as long as it does to obtain books directly from abroad, though some enterprising continental booksellers are now using air-freight for some shipments. Many booksellers in Western Europe use the container services offered by some forwarding agents in the UK: although this method of transport is less costly than the more traditional book post, it often takes longer. The cost of transport of imported books is usually studied very closely by the continental bookseller, as it can greatly influence his profit in this department

Many importing booksellers on the continental mainland of Europe maintain an interesting and representative stock of books in English within the fields of their interest. Perennial best-sellers such as *The Guinness book of records* are readily obtainable in season; the language section is certain to contain one or more of the Partridge titles on English slang; and the latest 'big name' novel in English will doubtless be available in the leading 'English' bookshops on the continent—thanks to the study, hard work and foresight of the multi-lingual buyers concerned.

Reading circles

Some continental bookshops run their own Reading Circles for books in the English language. This activity stimulates and promotes sales of books included in the lists of the Reading Circles and of other books which are not—but on a more limited scale than is possible in the UK, for example.

Interior shop design and layout

During the past few years the interiors of very many continental bookshops have been made more attractive, and at the same time more functional. These improvements have often been carried out at great cost, but have made the bookshops concerned much more welcoming and inviting. A common feature is the Information desk (usually manned by a very knowledgeable assistant) where the local, British, American, French, German, Italian, Spanish and other bibliographies are usually kept for reference; where customers' queries can be answered, and where customers' special orders can be placed. Book-displays are nowadays arranged to promote sales 'at sight'; at the same time permitting the maximum selection of suitable titles to be readily to hand on the nearby shelves, or in the drawers that are often found under the book-displays themselves.

Competing for space

One of the problems facing the importing continental bookseller is that of the space which can be given to books in the English language, especially during the tourist seasons. As it is costly to keep a large and perhaps slow-moving stock of books in a foreign language, it is inevitable that competition is keen as far as books in English are concerned. The vast output of books in English further heightens this competition, especially as the continental bookseller normally earns his bread and butter from the sale of locally-published books and often stationery too.

In general, however, importing continental booksellers are very much aware of the opportunities offered to them by British books, and have not been slow in giving books in English the same type of specialised treatment and attention that they often give to books in their own languages.

KEYNOTES

- The best foreign bookshops use active sales promotions to sell books. Publishers catalogues and subject lists are mailed to prospective customers. The telephone is also used to promote books or series.
- Continental bookshops often have information desks manned by a multilingual assistant.

13 LIBRARIES AND THE BOOKSHOP

By Frank Atkinson
Librarian, Cannon Street Library, City of London Library Service

BOOKSELLING IS DIFFERENT

It is difficult for a librarian to see how the average bookseller can make much of a living today. That, I suppose, is a poor way to start a contribution to a work on book sales promotion, but it's true. I mean, of course, a local independent bookseller—the owner of a real bookshop, not a dealer in everything from albums to yo-yos with a few titles on the side.

It was not always so. Twenty and some years ago, a young public librarian, frustrated by the limited opportunities in local government, might have thought wistfully of bookselling. He would have seen at that time the comfortable local bookseller, not only supported by a regular clientele, but also enjoying a close relationship with the chief librarian—and getting a good slice of the book fund. That, it should be remembered, was just for selling books.

In those days, chores such as accessioning, stamping, labelling and pocketing of books were called 'processing' and were part of the library assistant's job; moreover, the production of catalogue cards was an inner-sanctum mystery even to the majority of a library's staff.

The young librarians of those days have now reached unwistful middle-age and, with few exceptions, are still librarians. Some are chiefs, or even grander, with responsibility for the expenditure of book funds of Rockefeller proportions compared with those of the libraries of their youth. This responsibility may be delegated to a senior member of the staff—a bibliographical officer, stock editor, or some such—but, whoever it may be, he will almost certainly know the big library suppliers and their representatives better than he knows any local bookseller.

Library suppliers

The few major library supply firms are getting the lion's share of local authority book money. This is, perhaps, an inevitable result of the 'big business' trend in local government. These firms are giving good value for money. They are supplying books already 'serviced'–that is, labelled, pocketed, class-marked, plastic jacketed, and with typed book cards and catalogue cards. This servicing is done for what is called a nominal fee. Another way of putting it is to say that the library supplier is giving a discount well in excess of Library Licence ten per cent.

It is to be hoped that the small, independent bookseller will survive this crisis. The next part of this piece–how the local public librarian and the local bookseller can co-operate–is based on the belief that he *will* survive.

LIBRARIES AND BOOK TRADE COOPERATION

On a national level there is little–too little–contact between librarians and booksellers. From time to time there is a flurry of concern about this. The President of the Library Association, in a letter to the *Bookseller* (3 May 1975), stressed the need for closer contact and understanding between all people involved in libraries and the book trade. He pointed out that membership of the Library Association is open 'to all persons engaged in or interested in library work'.

Libtrad

Two weeks later, there was a letter in the same journal from Brian Baumfield, Chairman of the Working Party on Library and Book Trade Relations (LIBTRAD). He reminded readers of the working party's existence and of its ten years' work to improve relations between librarians and the book world. In addition, there is some out-of-hours fraternising at Library Association and other conferences, and a few annual dinner invitations. Yet all this touches no more than a small minority.

One journal in common

It is significant that the letters mentioned above appeared in the *Bookseller*. In spite of its title, it is the one periodical of equal interest to members of the book trade and librarians–and it is their longest-surviving common ground.

One hesitates to suggest, because of this, a change of title; but an innovation which would make it much easier to use initially and to consult in file form, *is* suggested—could there not be a contents list in each issue?

Local cooperation

The picture of re-organised local government is a depressing one for many booksellers (and for lots of other people too). It is, therefore, important to remember that, in spite of amalgamations and jumbo-sized departments and new titles for some chief officers, back at the coal-face the work still goes on. The local public library still functions.

The public librarian and the bookseller share the same book-minded section of the public. Despite a much-publicised contention to the contrary, they are not totally in competition. A book borrower is more likely to be a book buyer than is a person who never uses libraries. In fact, many a consistent book buyer uses the library facilities to assess the worth of a book before deciding to buy or not.

Writing in *New library world* (March 1975), Brian Griffin (who describes himself as an average user of the public library) went into some details of why and how he does this. 'The whole point of the process', he wrote, 'is that it enables me to explore books with as few extraneous pressures as possible. On these shelves the dead and the living, the obscure and the well-publicised, the high and the low-brow, exist in total democracy. All the froth of publicity, all the spurious solemnity is vanished . . . '

Publishers' publicity

We might stay with Griffin's image a moment to wonder if booksellers suffer as much as librarians do from the publishers' froth of publicity. I am thinking of the pamphlets, leaflets, dust-wrappers, letters and cards that spill daily on to our desks, puffing the same titles that are being advertised and reviewed in the newspapers and periodicals. Would it not be better that the money so spent should go to a Book Trade Promotion House for the production of general book publicity—seasonal posters and other display material for holidays, gardening, Christmas, and so on—the sort of stuff that is painstakingly churned out by enthusiastic amateurs in libraries throughout the country? This would show a better return to the book trade in general than the present mass of expensive, wastepaper basket fodder.

Benefits to be derived by the bookseller

The average branch library carries a stock of greater range and quantity than that of the neighbouring bookshop. Of course, it has the space and the funds to do this. Its rent and rates are paid and it doesn't have to make a profit. And yet there are benefits to be derived by the booksellers from this, should he so wish.

The public library is, in some degree, a shop window for the bookseller. Its resources of bibliographies and catalogues are available for identification of book titles and publication details. The library's accessions lists and other booklists should be of some interest to the bookseller, as should the book requests and other information on the public's reading requirements which accumulate at the Readers' Adviser's desk.

It is a regular occurrence for readers to ask at the library (some on their own initiative, some directed from booksellers) for confirmation, correction or amplification of brief details of books which they wish to buy. With equal regularity, a number return saying that the bookseller cannot supply some item or other which is in print. Now, to identify goods and to direct determined purchasers to a local dealer in those goods, would seem to be a useful service to the would-be buyer and a favour to the trader. But bookselling is different. Outside a comparatively narrow range of current, general publications, the attitude of a small percentage of bookshops is: 'If you don't see what you want, please don't ask for it'.

Booksellers' problems

Few people can be unaware of the booksellers' problems regarding single-copy and out-of-the-mainstream orders. We know also that they often feel ill-used by publishers' trade counters and backroom computers; and that Cassell and Collier Macmillan group's refusal of accounts worth less than £100 a year may start a trend. But something more than regretting the twenty year old loss of Simpkin Marshall, and bemoaning the shortcomings of the Book Centre, needs to be done. The threat of the supermarkets to the continued existence of the small grocers, gave rise to co-operative buying and distributing ventures such as Mace and Spar. Of course, bookselling is not the same as retail grocery, but the book trade is avidly adopting supermarket selling techniques for pushing books in general, so why not adopt or adapt other techniques so that specific, single-title orders would be welcome?

Librarians may not all, or always, live up to the maxim 'To every reader his book', but no request is lightly turned away. And, to this end, they have for many years co-operated in the buying, storing and interlending of books and other materials.

SELLING BOOKS IN PUBLIC LIBRARIES

There is, at the time of writing, some discussion about the selling of books in public libraries. At the LIBTRAD Holborn conference 1974, Robert Ashby (County Librarian of Surrey) wondered whether 'the idea of setting up a stall or shop inside a public library might not be explored further'. He foresaw some difficulties and cited the one of deciding which bookseller among a number should be favoured with the concession. Other obstacles are mentioned in an article by Lorna Paulin, until 1976 County Librarian of Hertfordshire (*The author*, Winter 1973). A shop run by a bookseller in the library 'would be unlikely to pay, unless the rent were heavily subsidised'. There would also be legal problems. Miss Paulin also dismisses the idea of a shop run by the library itself as unlikely to be financially self-supporting–'qualified library staff would be too expensive to devote to bookselling'.

Nevertheless, it is reported that public libraries in Hampshire may sell books in order to raise money, and the London Borough of Lambeth is considering a similar proposal. No doubt the Booksellers Association is in touch with local authority representatives and the Library Association about this?

Social amenity

To offer book buying facilities in public libraries as a social amenity, rather than as a means of raising money, is more likely to find favour with librarians and their committees. There was a proposal discussed at the 1973 Annual General Meeting of the Society of Authors, 'to extend the Public Library Service into bookselling as a self-supporting, non-profit making organisation . . .'

The proposer, Stephen Usherwood, intended that 'there would be no shop and no stock, only an order form similar to that for reserving books not on the shelves, and this form would be put through the library's normal buying machinery'.

The library as agent

This cuckoo-in-the-nest proposal was brought into manageable proportions by Lorna Paulin in her article quoted above. She suggested that the forms be passed to the local bookseller and that the library should claim a percentage of the turnover to cover expenses.

Orders, already confirmed as in-print, and with full bibliographical details, including SBN, would surely be welcomed by most booksellers. This scheme would also increase the number of people regularly using *both* libraries and bookshops to satisfy their total reading requirements.

Are there snags which the uncommercially-minded librarian cannot see? If not, why has this quite generous idea, propounded in *The author,* Winter 1973, not been seized upon and promoted by booksellers? Can a full life be all bestsellers?

KEYNOTES

- **A public library can be a shop window for a bookseller, too: it's stock is inevitably wider and larger than his.**
- **Should there be bookshops in public libraries? How would the concession be offered? Or could the library run it itself?**